The 7 Master Moves of Success

Jag Shoker

BENNION
KEARNY

To my son Dhyan.

Your arrival in this world brought with it the inspiration to complete this book.

I look forward to the day that you're old enough to read it and discover your own Ideal Way Forward in life.

Dear Bal,

I hope the words in this book encourage you to focus your mind on achieving what matters most to your heart,

Best wishes

Jag Dec '18

Acknowledgements

This book is a synthesis of many inspired ideas. I'm grateful to all the researchers, thinkers and writers quoted in this book who have dedicated their lives to gathering the specialist knowledge that has helped the rest of us to broaden our perspective on life and success.

The conceiving, researching, and writing of this book turned out to be a much larger and longer undertaking than I had first envisaged and I'm grateful specifically to:

My wife, Harj, for keeping your faith in me.

My parents, for showing me how to find that elusive balance between aspiration and contentment.

My dear friend, Paul Bassi, for your unfailing support at all times.

My dear friend, Yiannis Pittis, for your inspiration, wisdom, and foresight which helped to shape this book from the moment that it was no more than a small seed of an idea in my mind.

My dear friend, Terry Byrne, for agreeing to share your inspired story in this book.

And James Lumsden-Cook from Bennion Kearny, for your perceptiveness, challenge, and support in helping me to draft and redraft all the chapters within this book.

To all these individuals, I'd like to say, this book is infinitely better for your involvement.

About the Author

Jag Shoker is a leading performance coach and the founder of Inspired Movement™ - a high performance coaching and consultancy business for business leaders, sports professionals, and creative performers.

Drawing upon an extensive background in both business and performance coaching, Jag uses his unique Inspired Movement performance model to help talented individuals and progressive organisations to achieve greater success.

Jag is also an engaging and energising motivational speaker who shares his deep understanding of the principles behind success and high performance with a diverse range of audiences.

Contents

Success Moves

The moves we make

In the rare moments of stillness and silence that we manage to secure in our busy lives, a hard fact about life dawns upon us. That fact is this: *life compels us to move*. None of us are exempt from this fate.

Life demands that we act and react to events as they unfold around us. We must "do or die". We must play the game of life or watch as it slips through our hands. This is true as much for those who seek to do the bare minimum to get by, as it is for those driven individuals leading the vanguard of progress.

Whether you desire security or the highest levels of self-expression in your life and work, success depends upon your ability to find the optimal courses of action or the *right moves*. As this book endeavours to show you, successful individuals in any sphere possess a defining quality: *they know what moves to make and crucially when and how to make them.*

The moves we make through life very much define us. As many books and seminars that have explored success point out, *success is not a destination it is a journey*; one in which we must keep moving towards an ideal. It is a journey that involves many progressive steps. On occasions it demands that we stride forward courageously and at speed. At other times it requires us to stop where we are, and reflect, and decide if there is a better direction in which to head, a better way in which to move or if there is a better course of action to take. At critical junctures in this journey we may have to take a leap of faith and find the self-belief that is needed to jump across the dark chasm that separates the known from the unknown, if we want to achieve something of significance and note.

The relentless requirement to keep moving, however, can and has made many of us wary. The psychiatrist Edward Hallowell, in his article *Overloaded Circuits*, for example, described the problem facing frenzied business executives working in 'hyperkinetic environments'. Hallowell wrote:

They're suffering from a newly recognized neurological phenomenon called Attention Deficit Trait (ADT). Marked by distractibility, inner frenzy, and impatience, ADT prevents managers from clarifying priorities, making smart decisions, and managing their time. This insidious condition turns otherwise talented performers into harried underachievers. And it's reaching epidemic proportions. [1]

The regular walk, train, or car journey into work which brings us face-to-face with a sea of stressed and anxious faces gives credence to Hallowell's claims. Driven by more advanced and efficient technology, life seems to be getting faster – and it appears as though we are struggling to keep pace.

Back in 1937, in his book *Great Contemporaries*, Winston Churchill wrote: "...the world is moving on; and moving so fast that few have time to ask – whither?" Over 75 years further on, we can say with absolute certainty that life is moving quicker still and many of us really do not have the time to ask in which direction our lives are inexorably moving.

Life demands that we move.
Success demands that we make the right move.

Information, ideas, conversations are exchanged so quickly through mobile phones, emails and social media that the "state of play" is always rapidly changing. Events compel us to stick with the pace and cope with the pressure, or else, fall by the wayside.

Staying the course

With our physical capacities seemingly being stretched to their limit, how can we survive with the demands life imposes on us? I believe the fast paced and highly pressurised world of professional sport provides a compelling answer to this question, particularly if we examine the 'unlikely' success of three individuals who were considered by many to be the greatest sportsmen of their generation in their respective sports - Muhammad Ali, Wayne Gretzky and Zinedine Zidane.

Ali was renowned for his speed but he wasn't considered by many boxing experts to be a natural fighter or one that had the physique, strength or the correct style of a classic heavy-weight boxer; and yet as one boxing expert explained:

He was a paradox. His physical performances in the ring were absolutely wrong... Yet his brain was always in perfect working condition... He showed us all that all victories come from here, [hitting his forehead with his index finger, then raising a pair of fists]: Not from here. [2]

Gretzky, like Ali, didn't have a physique that appeared to be able to withstand the cut and thrust of professional ice-hockey. When in the 1981-82 season, he broke the National Hockey League record by scoring 92 goals, his build was slight compared to the average NHL player. In fact, as he described himself, "I look more like the guy who bags your groceries at the local supermarket." [3] However, as one

3

journalist wrote, Gretzky could do something a little quicker than nearly all other players:

Gretzky doesn't look like a hockey player... his shot is only average – or, nowadays, below average... Gretzky's gift, his genius even, is for seeing...To most fans, and sometimes even to the players on the ice, hockey frequently looks like chaos... But amid the mayhem, Gretzky can discern the game's underlying pattern and flow, and anticipate what's going to happen faster and in more detail than anyone else in the building. [4]

Zidane, was another great sportsman, who was able to overcome a physical limitation; as the author Jonathan Wilson revealed in *Inverting the Pyramid* (his insightful take on football philosophy), the French coach Aimé Jacquet had to find a way of accommodating Zidane in his 1998 World Cup winning side on account of Zidane being "a player of limited pace and almost no defensive instinct". [5] However, in an interview with a journalist, Jacquet explained what made Zidane so special:

Zidane has an internal vision. His control is precise and discreet. He can make the ball do whatever he wants. But it is his drive which takes him forward. He is 100 per cent football. [6]

The Latin motto of the Olympic Games, *altius, citius, fortius,* – higher, faster, stronger – suggests that success in sport weighs heavily in the favour of supreme athletes. Yet despite their purported physical disadvantages, Ali, Gretzky and Zidane were not only able to survive in the fast moving and demanding arenas of their respective sports, *they were able to flourish.* They found a way of out-competing physically superior opposition.

The ability to compete and succeed in a fast-moving world flows, first and foremost, from what we possess within us.

The qualities shown by these three men are not the sole preserve of sports stars or athletes. Exceptional individuals in other walks of life are also able to compete with bigger and stronger opponents, with qualities that run deeper than physical attributes.

Alexander the Great, for example, lacked an imposing physical presence due to his lack of height; a quality that was revered in ancient times. However, despite the inches he gave away in height, he became one of history's greatest military leaders due to his ability to make decisive moves amidst the chaos of a battlefield.[7] History notes that Napoleon, another leader of modest physical stature, also possessed similar qualities to Alexander the Great; qualities that secured victory after victory. As Malcolm Gladwell wrote in his book *Blink*:

In the military, brilliant generals are said to possess "coup d'oeil" – which translated from the French, means "power of the glance": the ability to immediately see and make sense of the battlefield. Napoleon had coup d'oeil.

Another celebrated leader - Mahatma Gandhi - also found the right moves to see off more powerful opposition; Gandhi was able to defeat the might of the British Empire through his strategy of *satyagraha*, or passive resistance, through the moral integrity of his character. As Albert Einstein, speaking at the time of Gandhi's death, pointed out:

Gandhi had demonstrated that a powerful human following can be assembled not only through the cunning game of usual political manoeuvres and trickeries but through the cogent example of a morally superior conduct of life. [8]

So, what lay behind the respective successes of Ali, Gretzky, Zidane, Alexander, Napoleon and Gandhi? They all had an ability to *outmanoeuvre* more powerful opponents. They knew what moves to make and when and how to make them with maximum effect. It is an ability that the ancient Greeks of Alexander's time, referred to as *phronesis*, or practical wisdom. [9] Gladwell explained it is the kind of knowledge that helps you read situations correctly and get what you want.[10]

All these exceptional individuals had a practical intelligence that allowed them to read the game or situations before them and make the right moves that created the success or outcomes they desired. I call this ability *Inspired Movement*. Exceptional individuals who possess it – as Ali, Gretzky, Zidane, Alexander, Napoleon and Gandhi did – are what I refer to, in this book, as Inspired Movers.

---

*An Inspired Mover is someone who can perceive
and perform the moves that create the desired
success in any situation.*

The brief insights into these Inspired Movers immediately point to one thing. They could *out-think* their opponents. Ali's victories came from "his brain and not his fists". Gretzky's came from an "anticipation of what was going to happen faster than anyone else". Zidane's came from an "internal vision". Alexander and Napoleon built their victories on the power of perception or "coup d'oeil". Gandhi ultimately defeated the British Empire with a subtly conceived strategy of passive resistance.

All these cases of Inspired Movement show that the abilities to think well and move well are intimately linked. However, if we were to look for a practical and workable definition of Inspired Movement, the ability 'to think' only represents half the equation. For the other vital element, let's turn to another of history's Inspired Movers.

The art and science of Inspired Movement

He became one of the cultural icons of the 20th century. A man whose ability to move and express himself mesmerised film audiences in the East and the West. Many considered him to be one of the most influential and talented martial artists of all time. Sadly, Bruce Lee's life was prematurely cut short when he died in 1973, aged only 32, from a cerebral oedema brought on by an allergic reaction to pain medication he had taken.

In 1994, an interview that he gave on the Pierre Berton Show (two years before his death) was found and aired on television for the very first time. In the interview Bruce Lee spoke of his martial arts philosophy. "Empty your mind. Be formless, shapeless like water," he said leaning forward towards a captivated Pierre Berton. "Put water into a cup and it becomes the cup. Put water into the bottle and it becomes the bottle. Put it into a teapot, it becomes the teapot. Water can flow or it can crash. Be water my friend."

The words may sound quixotic but Lee's philosophy helped him to move with exceptional power and poise. As he further elaborated, "Here is natural instinct and here is control. You are to combine the two in harmony," he said making fists with both hands before bringing them together before him, "...If you have one to the extreme you'll be *very unscientific*. If you have another to the extreme you become all of a sudden a *mechanical man*, no longer a human being."

Lee's style of moving and expressing himself was both practical and philosophical. A style that was balanced between nature and nurture. It represents the sine qua non of Inspired Movement; making the right moves is the convergence of science *and art*, of thought *and emotion*. Too much thought (control) and we run the danger of becoming the contrived "mechanical man" that makes moves without any joy or feeling. Too much emotion, however, and we run the danger of losing our head and moving capriciously without care. As Konstantin Stanislavski, the famous Russian actor and theatre director said:

...we need science but we must be intelligent and forehanded about acquiring it. There is no point in filling our heads with a lot of new ideas and rushing on the stage to exploit them before we have learned the elementary rules. That kind of a student will lose his head, he will either forget his science or think about it to the exclusion of everything else. Science can help art only when they support and complement each other. [11]

The power of emotion, alongside thought, is especially required when the right moves in any situation require *passionate and expansive* action. As Nelson Mandela once said, "There is no passion to be found playing small – in settling for a life that is less than the one you are capable of living." To play a bigger game in life requires us to move with greater passion and feeling as well as thought and perception.

To find our best form, we must find a balance between science and art - of what we know and how we feel - for thought and feeling are instrumental in how we express ourselves. They are the two forces

7

that *literally* move us. For example, the word emotion, is derived from a Latin verb *movere* which means *to move*. The word motivation, is also linked to the concept of moving; motivation implies we have a *motive* or a *sponsoring thought* behind doing something.

Thought is the power that directs and shapes the moves we make. Emotion is the power that energises and empowers them. Inspired Movement therefore is very much *a high thinking and high feeling state* in which sublime thoughts blend perfectly with sublime feelings to create exceptional performance.

Mastering Inspired Movement – the ability to make the right move in any situation – therefore, requires an approach which is as much 'heart' as it is 'head'.

Inspired Movement is unleashed when thought and feeling combine. When the head and the heart work with equal power.

In my experience, putting aside any specific technical or physical ability, people too frequently attribute success solely to a strong 'mindset'. This can make the pursuit of exceptional performance feel like a dry or mechanical exercise in thinking better. It is this bias of 'thinking *over* feeling' instead of 'thinking *with* feeling' that I believe causes so many individuals to fall out of love with their profession and experience poor performance in their work.

To correct the balance we perhaps need to add the term 'heart-set' to that of mindset, in the vocabulary of success - and provide a more holistic view on personal performance. A strong heart-set would include essential qualities such as courage, love and belief that are required to *ignite* the potential of a strong mindset.

The role the heart and emotions plays in success is, in fact, receiving greater attention by both academics and those more practically engaged in the pursuit of success. As the highly influential ex-CEO of Apple, the late Steve Jobs, pointed out: "…most important, have the courage to follow your heart and intuition. They somehow already know what you truly want to become. Everything else is secondary."

As we'll come to, later in the book, the heart has a tangible role to play in human performance and decision making. For now, however, let's consider how we can combine the power of thought and emotion into a *practical definition of Inspired Movement.*

Defining Inspired Movement

The personal excellence demonstrated by Inspired Movers makes them stand-out from the crowd. There is even a defining difference between them and individuals working within the same field who are considered to be 'merely' good as opposed to great. The current so called 'Big Four' players in men's tennis are a great example of this. Roger Federer, Rafael Nadal, Novak Djokovic and Andy Murray have (between them) won 34 of the last 35 Grand Slam men's singles titles. But what exactly is the defining difference between them and the rest? Djokovic puts the gap in success between the Big Four and the chasing pack down to *greater mental strength and emotional stability* in crucial moments in matches. [12]

Knowing exactly how Inspired Movers create and combine mental and emotional strength, however, can be a challenging and elusive task. Peak human performance is not the sole preserve of any one discipline. It touches many areas such as psychology, neuroscience, physiology, leadership, as well as religion, philosophy and spirituality. Given the fact that the potential causes of Inspired Movement are so wide-ranging, can we nonetheless devise a useful definition for it?

I believe we can but it requires us to adopt what Howard Gardner, the Harvard Professor and one of the world's foremost thinkers in education, calls a *Synthesizing Mind.* [13] Gardner states that the amount of accumulated knowledge is reportedly doubling every two to three years. Sources of information have become so widespread and disparate that we desperately need to combine and connect complex ideas. We need to *synthesise* all relevant information into a wider coherent pattern. Put simply we need to make sure we can see the bigger picture without losing sight of the useful knowledge that is surfacing all the time, from all directions.

*High Performance is a synthesis of many
disciplines and ideas. Success flows when
all our attributes come together
and combine harmoniously.*

Within this book, the definition for Inspired Movement that I share
with you, is a product of the years of high performance coaching I
have provided to my clients and the parallel research I have
undertaken into the vast field of human potential. Through
'synthesizing' the experiences gained and the knowledge gathered, I
devised the definition – which contains the potential to dynamically
shift your personal performance – by repeatedly asking myself the
following two questions:

- What defines human excellence?

- What factors bring it about?

Following Einstein's wisdom that "everything should be made as
simple as possible, but not simpler" I have defined Inspired
Movement in the simplest possible terms:

*Inspired Movement is the ability to make the optimal moves at the right time and
the right place, in any situation, by moving in complete alignment with the Ideal
Way Forward.*

The first component of the Inspired Movement definition is the
success trait that all top performers possess - that we have alluded to
in this opening chapter of this book. It is the enhanced decision
making and execution capability of making the optimal moves in any
situation. Inspired Movers consistently know what moves to make
and when and how to make them. Top sports stars like Roger
Federer know when to defend and when to attack; perceptive
investors such as Warren Buffet know when it is time to "be fearful
when others are greedy and be greedy when others are fearful";
exceptional entrepreneurs like Richard Branson know when to say
"screw it let's do it" and when to hold back a product; and great

authors like J.K. Rowling know what to say and what to leave to the imagination.

Possessing the right moves is the key to all success.

That is not to say Inspired Movers do not make wrong, ill-timed or sub-optimal moves. Like all of us they can find themselves 'off-track' in situations that challenge their values, purpose and aspirations. When Inspired Movers do err, however, they find a move that quickly gets them back on track. Typically they find the optimal moves when they are most required. This task of finding the right moves in any situation is the opportunity and challenge that very much confronts us all.

However, none of us make the same moves in the same way. Despite the fact that biologists claim that only 0.1% of our DNA separates us from each other, [14] we each think, feel and act in remarkably different ways. This uniqueness in the way each of us moves is reflected in the second component of the Inspired Movement definition; it's not just what we do (or the moves we make), it's the *way we do it* that gives each of us our own natural form of self-expression.

Inspired Movers have discovered what I call their own *Ideal Way Forward* in life. They move in a way that *feels* right to them. As I describe later, the Ideal Way Forward represents the moves that best serve their purpose and are most true to their values. In essence, *Inspired Movers express who they choose to be through what they choose to do.* To use sporting greats as an analogy – in football where Pelé skilfully combined with his teammates, Maradona terrorised opponents with individual flair; in tennis, where Roger Federer's game is built on graceful elegance and precision, Rafael Nadal's is built on muscular power and determination; in athletics where the US sprinter Allyson Felix glides gracefully on the track, her great rival Veronica Campbell-Brown sprints with explosive power. As Ralph Waldo Emerson eloquently pointed out in his essay, *Self-Reliance,* each of us must find our unique expression:

Insist on yourself, never imitate. Your own gift you can present every moment with the cumulative force of a whole life's cultivation; but of the adopted talent of another, you have only an extemporaneous half possession.

11

We must fashion an Ideal Way Forward that is unique and authentic to each of us. Our moves must flow naturally from within.

The Seven Master Moves of Success

The Inspired Movement definition can be stated simply enough, but how can we practically use it to create the success we desire? The answer lies in the *Seven Master Moves* that are embedded into the definition of Inspired Movement that spark it into life. As shown in Figure 1.1 they are the ability to move with:

1. Progression

2. Purpose

3. Passion

4. Presence

5. Precision

6. Perception

7. Poise

Perform The Optimal Moves
[Precision and Poise]

at

The Right Time, Right Place
[Perception]

with

Complete Alignment
[Passion and Presence]

to

The Ideal Way Forward
[Purpose and Progression]

Figure 1.1, The 7 Master Moves of Inspired Movement

These Seven Master Moves are powerful forces that channel you in the direction of success. As this book will explore, your Ideal Way Forward will compel you to move with *purpose and progression.* It will stir your heart into action. You will *passionately* desire to follow its direction. It will challenge and test you, and bring out a commanding *presence* within you that will give you the courage that is needed to find your own way and the self-belief that is needed to persevere on this path; for the path of self-mastery is necessarily long. It is the price that must be paid for success.

Moving with greater freedom and *precision* requires many thousands of hours of painstaking practice. The effortless unleashing of your repertoire of moves can only be acquired, ironically, through *great effort.* Knowing when, and where, to make your move will require a refined sense of *perception.* Being able to make your move, and make it count in the critical moments upon which your future rests, will require the kind of unshakable *poise* that can only be developed when the very limits of your ability and character are repeatedly tested.

Each chapter that follows explores each of the Seven Master Moves in turn. However, reading the chapters is not enough. You must, in your own way, embody any knowledge that resonates within you. The performance principles shared within these pages, have to be applied to gain any value from them. Inspiration must be turned into application if you are to create the success you deeply desire in your life.

To help this process, I have included a section entitled *'Applying the Master Move'* at the end of each chapter. These sections contain practical information and exercises that can help you create a dynamic shift in your personal performance. They are not 'how to' lists though; even if someone with great foresight could spell out the precise steps for you to follow (in your personal pursuit of the Ideal Way Forward) I do not believe that following this path would ultimately be beneficial for you. Books, friends and 'experts' can, and do, play important roles in guiding, prompting and inspiring us. We should not, however, overlook the deep instinct within us, or the joy to be had for that matter, *of working things out for ourselves.*

Our inspiration must inform and drive our application. Knowledge brings success when it is intelligently and passionately applied.

Most importantly, do not be tempted to rush through any exercises shared in this book or to be put off by their simplicity. As with all things, reliable and repeated practice will yield great results *in time.*

This book is not about changing your life miraculously in seven days. A lifetime's worth of habits and conditioning cannot be overturned so easily. As I explain to my clients, changing how you think, how you feel, and how you move *is possible* but it requires real sustained effort. If you earnestly read and act upon the words written within this book, the Seven Master Moves will help you to:

- Manifest the success you desire.

- Perform with greater courage, belief and confidence.

- Move with greater motivation, skill and clarity.

Before you begin turning the pages of the second part of this book, however, know that creating success and mastering your own fate is exceptionally rewarding but it is hard work and no-one else can do the work for you. As Orison Swett Marden writes in *Pushing to the Front,* a classic book on personal success, "There is no open door to the temple of success. Everyone who enters makes his own door, which closes behind him to all others, not even permitting his own children to pass."

Great effort enables Inspired Movers to move with greater power and influence than the rest. If you would like to move as they do, this book will help show you the way; but if you haven't already done so, make the firm commitment to yourself that your journey towards success starts *here* and *now.*

There is only one way to know what is really possible in your life:

Discover your Ideal Way Forward and stride intelligently and courageously towards it until the success you desire is yours to enjoy.

Let's begin.

---

[1] Hallowell, E.M., *Overloaded Circuits in HBR 10 Must Reads: On Managing Yourself,* Boston, Harvard Business Review Press, 2010, p69.

[2] Dennis, F., & Atyeo, D., *Muhammad Ali: The Glory Years,* New York, Hyperion, 2003, p14.

[3] Ranadive, V & Maney, K., *The Two-Second Advantage,* London, Hodder, 2011, p3.

[4] McGrath, C., New York Times Magazine, March 13, 1997.

[5] Wilson, J., *Inverting the Pyramid – A History of Football Tactics,* London, Orion Books, 2008, p.345.

[6] Hussey, A., *ZZ Top,* The Observer, April 4 2004

[7] See Adair, J., *Effective Leadership Masterclass,* London, Pan Books, 2010 edition, p44-45

[8] Fisher, L., *The Life of Mahatma Gandhi,* London, HarperCollins 1997.

[9] See Adair, J., *Effective Leadership Masterclass,* London, Pan Books, 2010 edition, p44-45

[10] Gladwell, M., *Outliers,* London, Penguin, p101.

[11] Stanislavski, K., *Building a Character,* London, Methuen Drama, 2008 (first published in Great Britain in 1950), p110.

[12] On article featured on the official ATP World Tour website, *Djokovic: "There's definitely a gap",* May 5th 2013:
http://www.atpworldtour.com/News/Tennis/2013/05/19/Madrid-Djokovic-Preview.aspx

[13] Gardner, H., *5 Minds for the Future,* Boston, Harvard Business Press, 2008.

[14] Statistic on DNA quoted in *Harvard Business Review 10 Must Reads: On Strategy,* Boston, Harvard Business Review Press, 2011, p205

Master Move 1
Move with Progression

Transformation in time

Intensive mastery

The price to be paid

The myth of rapid success

Ever upward progress

Hope and false hope

Self-help promises

Inspired Movers know more is possible. The Ideal Way Forward is mastered progressively in time.

Limitless?

In 2011, an American science-fiction movie called *Limitless* (starring Bradley Cooper and Robert De Niro) was released which explored an interesting premise: what if you could access one hundred percent of your brain's potential to become a perfect version of yourself? That is what happens to the film's lead character, Eddie Morra (played by Cooper), who is a struggling author suffering from a bad case of writer's block.

His fortunes change suddenly, however, when he takes an untested 'smart drug' called NZT which gives him instant access to his full potential. With his brain working at full capacity he can suddenly remember everything he has ever read, seen or heard, he can learn any new language in the space of days, his brain can compute complex mathematics effortlessly and he can impress anyone he meets with a new found conversational brilliance. Inspired by his NZT induced reality, Eddie finishes what proves to be a best-selling book in what seems like no time at all, turns a small investment stake on Wall Street into millions in the space of a few days, and attracts the attention of one of Wall Street's richest men, Carl Van Loon (played by De Niro), who despite being sceptical and hard to please, asks Morra to broker one of the largest mergers in corporate history.

What if, as the movie suggests, you can rapidly tap into an inner brilliance? What if anything is suddenly possible? What dreams would you entertain? What would you attempt to achieve in life if you discovered you had all the right moves for any given situation?

The idea of limitless potential and rapid success is an intoxicating one and has been the central message and promise of many self-help books. Its appeal has certainly captivated a large and receptive global audience. It is reported that the burgeoning self-help industry is worth an estimated $11billion in the United States alone. [1]

Rhonda Byrne's best-selling book *The Secret* which has sold an estimated 19 million copies world-wide (translated into 46 languages) typifies many of the leading books of the success/self-help genre. It claims that we can *attract all the happiness, health and success we desire* through a positive mindset and an unwavering belief in a beneficent and infinitely intelligent Universe. A Universe that can supply all the abundance we seek.

In the book Byrne writes that "a shortcut to manifesting your desires is to see what you want as an absolute fact." [2] To support her claim she quotes the verse Mark 11:24 from the Bible: "What things soever ye desire, when ye pray, believe that ye receive them, and ye shall have them." She also shares the thoughts of a handful of contemporary philosophers, metaphysicians, psychologists and entrepreneurs who support her belief in the immutable "law of attraction" and who make various assertions such as "The Universe knows the shortest, quickest, fastest, most harmonious way between you and your dreams."; "Whatever the mind can conceive it can achieve."; and "Whatever we think about and thank about we bring about."

The promise of the book, and of the positive psychology movement in general, is similar to that of the drug NZT in *Limitless:* firstly that *anything is possible* and secondly that there is a definite *short-cut to creating success.*

But can we rely on these two principle claims? This is an important question and one that is the focus of the First Master Move; if we are to move progressively – to follow the Ideal Way Forward in our lives or careers – should we believe in limitless potential and rapid success?

As we discussed in part one of the book, the Ideal Way Forward is the unique direction that every would-be Inspired Mover must discover for themselves. It is the form of *personal* success we desire most. As we shall explore in each of the following Master Moves the Ideal Way Forward represents *what we want to achieve* through expressing *who we choose to be*. It is *the course of action that best serves our purpose and is most true to our values.*

---

*To move progressively is to follow the Ideal Way
Forward and to pursue our purpose whilst
remaining true to our values.*

And so, coming back to the promise of limitless potential and rapid success, if we hope to unleash the power of Inspired Movement:

- *What should we believe is possible in life?*

- *How rapidly can we expect to master the optimal moves that can create the success we desire?*

Let's move forward by exploring the first of these two questions.

What should we believe is possible?

When we aim high in life, we sense a world of greater possibility that excites us. We experience a burst of highly motivated energy which carries us forward on a wave of optimism. We become hopeful that our best achievements and highest attainments lie ahead of us. This hope is a quintessential human quality. It provides the heart and determination that is needed to succeed in life; as the 17th century English scholar and preacher, Thomas Fuller said, "If it were not for hope, the heart would break."

It is hope in a better future, in greater possibilities and a seemingly infinite potential that underlies much of the self-help industry's promise. However, hope or *false-hope* can, according to some, be highly damaging; as the philosopher Nietzsche declared, "Hope is the worst of evils for it prolongs the torment of man."

When our hopes are not realised they can cause strong disillusionment; a point which has been picked up by critics of the self-help/positive psychology movement, who vehemently question the 'grandiose' claims of advocates, and the good they actually do.

In his book *SHAM* (an acronym coined by its author for the term 'Self-Help and Actualization Movement') Steve Salerno writes about the potential harm positive psychology books may do to individuals who buy them. Individuals who are lured in by the grand promises of transformation, happiness and success but who ultimately fail to achieve their aims because they did not *"believe enough"* in their dream or potential.

Like Salerno, Barbara Ehrenreich, the author of the book *Bright-Sided*, writes about the downside of America's penchant for positive thinking which she claims on a personal level has led to increasing self-blame and a morbid preoccupation with stamping out 'negative' thoughts; and on a national level which has created an era of irrational optimism which has contributed to the financial crisis which has afflicted the global economy since 2008.

However, the self-help industry is not the sole cause of false hope. In his excellent book *Thinking Fast and Slow* the Nobel prizing winning author, Daniel Kahneman, outlined the danger of what he refers to as the "optimistic bias" that many of us possess in our thinking:

Most of us view the world as more benign than it really is, our attributes as more favorable than they truly are, and the goals we adopt as more achievable than they are likely to be. We also tend to exaggerate our ability to forecast the future, which fosters optimistic overconfidence[3].

In the book, Kahneman gives the example of "entrepreneurial delusions" that many business owners entertain. He states that the chance of a small business surviving for five years in the United States is about 35% but most new business owners do not believe that the statistic applies to them. Kahneman quotes a survey of American entrepreneurs in which 81% put their personal odds of success at 7 out of 10 or higher, and 33% said their chance of failing was zero.

Irrational optimism may also surface from sources closer to home for many of us, namely *our parents*, especially those that psychologists refer to as the *"philoprogenitive type"* who typically believe their children are more attractive or talented than others. These parents have a strong tendency to over-praise their offspring, which can lead to bitter disappointment later, and discouragement, if their children realise (in the harsh professional reality of say business or sport) that they are not as good as they were led to believe and that a great deal more work is required to plug the gap between them and the best within their field.

A fine line must be trod between hope and false hope if we are not to lose our way or lose our heart.

The potential disillusionment, and the discouragement that false hope brings, is a genuine problem that can derail our attempts to progressively move forward. It is important, therefore, that self-help or success books (like the one you hold in your hands) do not oversell their promise. However, whilst I do believe there is a case to be made that some self-help authors or gurus have been prone to a degree of enthusiastic hyperbole – causing dissatisfaction and dejection amongst their readers who haven't achieved the scale of success they desired – I think *hope* plays a hugely important role in convincing us that individually and collectively, we can all strive to be more and do more. Hope in a better future is something, I believe, we should nurture, especially as there is much in life which suggests that human capabilities are ever-improving. Whilst the more enthusiastic and optimistic amongst us may claim that *anything is possible* in life, this book and the Seven Master Moves are based around a different premise and that is: we should believe that *more is possible in life*.

Onwards and upwards

In the short space of the last hundred years, in particular, our lives have been transformed by advances in technology that amaze us with their sophistication. More is becoming possible each day. Products such as cars, mobile phones and computers continue to evolve and astonish us with their capability.

A great example of this was illustrated in a TED Conference talk given by a human-computer interface designer called Jeff Han in February 2006.[4] In the talk, Han demonstrated publicly, for the first time, the touch screen technology that we now take for granted on our mobile phones, tablets, and laptops. When Han touched his screen and made the objects on it move the audience whistled, clapped and gasped out aloud in sheer amazement. For the likes of Apple and Samsung, the Ideal Way Forward changed in that minute – suddenly more was possible.

The same is true for so much technological innovation. The 2013 Frankfurt Motor Show, for example, saw the launch of the BMW i8, the company's first electric plug-in hybrid sports car. The BMW i8 hits 0 to 62mph in 4.4 seconds, does 155mph, and has an impressive engine output of 362bhp. Remarkably this performance is achieved with emissions of only 59g/km of CO_2 and a quoted fuel efficiency of 113mpg. The i8 heralds a new direction for the company. They are pursuing an Ideal Way Forward that combines exceptional performance *with* exceptional efficiency.

Ten years ago few would have believed you could get supercar performance with the supermini efficiency that the i8 delivers; a decade or so ago, certainly, few of us would have believed in the power of touch screen technology that Han demonstrated in 2006, and yet now it is commonplace. Sitting behind these technological innovations is a human capability and ingenuity that continues to evolve. In all fields, Inspired Movers are leading the way and revealing that more is possible.

Consider the success of Warren Buffet, one of the world's richest individuals and one of its most successful investors. Buffet is the primary shareholder, chairman and chief executive of Berkshire Hathaway, a US company which he took over in 1965. As reported by one financial journalist, "A $10,000 investment in Berkshire Hathaway stock in 1965 would have grown to be worth nearly $30 million 40 years later, in 2005. That's about *60 times* as much as you would have made if you'd invested $10,000 in the Standard & Poor's 500 Index and held it for those same 40 years." [5] Buffet's success is the reason why investors small and big alike track his every foray into the stock market: the Ideal Way Forward he has pursued has stretched the possibilities of success. Buffett has found a way of consistently making the right moves which have made others believe that more is possible.

In the world of business, *Fortune's* Senior Editor-at-Large, Geoff Colvin, reports that it has become possible in recent years to create great levels of shareholder wealth through new types of business models that rely less (relatively speaking) on financial capital but more on human capital and capability.[6]

For example, Microsoft has managed to create about $221 billion of shareholder wealth from about $30 billion of financial capital and Google has created about $124 billion of shareholder wealth from $5 billion of capital. By contrast, PepsiCo and Procter & Gamble, two more traditional yet still excellently run companies have only generated about $73 billion and $126 billion of shareholder wealth respectively, with PepsiCo using about $34 billion of financial capital and Proctor & Gamble about $83 billion. Companies like Microsoft and Google have *leveraged the human capital* they possess to achieve greater possibilities and wealth creation. Both companies have reputations for only hiring the most talented minds; these individuals collectively mastermind the Ideal Way Forward for these companies allowing them to surpass expectations.

If Inspired Movers in business are going further, so too are Inspired Movers in sport. They are making better and more powerful moves year on year. At one time, for example, 10 seconds represented both a physical and psychological barrier to male sprinters competing in the 100 metre sprint. However, since Jim Hines recorded the first-ever non-wind assisted sub-10 second performance in 1968, over 86 sprinters in total have broken the 10-second barrier with an official legally recorded time; [7] and the fastest man in the world, Usain Bolt, has taken the event even further to almost unimaginable heights. Bolt has altered many people's perception of what is humanly possible in the sport. At the 2009 World Championships in Berlin he posted a world record performance of 9.58 seconds which astounded the world of athletics.

Remarkably, it seems Bolt could go even faster. Michael Johnson, himself one of the sport's greatest sprinters, believes that Bolt could potentially run a time of 9.40 seconds if, biomechanically speaking, he sharpens up the combination of moves he typically unleashes during the different phases of a 100 metre race.[8] Even for Bolt – who we could consider to be an ultimate Inspired Mover – more is still possible.

As Inspired Movers continue to shift performance boundaries to higher levels they are pulling their closest competitors along with them. When Bolt won the 100 metre final at the London Olympics, breaking the Olympic record in the process, only one of the eight sprinters failed to sprint the distance in under ten seconds. And when Roger Bannister famously ran the first ever sub-four minute mile, several other runners managed the same feat within the following two years.[9] In fact, as the research of Anders Ericsson, one of the world's leading authorities on expert performance, has shown, in nearly every aspect of human endeavour there have been increases in the efficiency and level of performance through greater knowledge and know-how. [10]

In academia, Roger Bacon the thirteenth century English Scholar, believed it would impossible to master mathematics in a time span of less than 30 to 40 years; today a similar level of calculus is taught to almost all college students.

In music, modern day piano and violin performers are able to master music that was considered unplayable by the leading musicians in the 19th century. Modern day performers are even able to match and occasionally go beyond the technical brilliance displayed by the likes of Mozart.

In sport, Ericsson reports that Olympic swimmers in the previous century would fail to qualify for swim teams in today's most competitive *college* teams. In athletics we see a similar story. At the 1908 Olympics the 200 meters final was won in a time of 22.60 seconds; the current US high school record is a whole two seconds faster. Likewise, the present US high school record for the marathon is a significant 20 minutes faster than the winning time recorded for the event at the 1908 Olympics.

The wealth of performance data across all aspects of life is pointing to one thing: collectively as a race, we are *moving with greater progression*. The Ideal Way Forward, across all domains, is growing more sophisticated. The moves we are making are becoming more efficient, complex and powerful. To the great human virtue of hope we are adding knowledge which is enhancing the possibilities for us all. Innovations in technology such as the touch screen technology and electric cars are growing as we continue to build on what we know. Inspired Movers in business and sport are not just shifting the limits of what is possible through hope alone – better insights, better knowledge, and enhanced training methods are giving our feeling of hope in a better future real power and momentum.

When knowledge is added to hope,
more becomes possible.

It seems reasonable and fair, therefore, to believe that with greater hope and knowledge more is possible for each of us; especially – as we shall see at different stages within this book – our growing understanding of the human brain is unearthing some remarkable findings that would not be out of place in the world of science fiction. For example, the 'way we think' literally changes the brain's physical shape and inherent potential. The fact that our brains can change means that we can too, and that opens out the possibilities for us all.

However, even with this level-headed belief that more is possible, there is still a danger that our hopes could lead to disillusionment; as I regularly experience first-hand through my work – individuals can become disheartened (and sceptical about transformational change) when the changes they desire do not manifest in the *short time-scales* they expect. This leads us back to the other key focus of this Master Move:

How rapidly can we expect to master the optimal moves that can create the success we desire?

The myth of sudden success

For a largely impatient world, such as ours, that demands instant success, the idea of rapid change holds massive appeal, and helps to explain why so many spend so much money on self-improvement each year. The belief in rapid success has dominated much of our thinking in recent years but it is, in my opinion, an intoxicating idea that leads to greater harm and false hope. Despite much evidence suggesting otherwise, a belief in rapid success continues to hold much sway over our thinking.

The first reason for this – and something which we will explore in more detail in the next Master Move – is that many define success by what they own and possess; what they 'have' shapes how they, and others like them, perceive how successful they are. Before the financial crisis of 2008 I believe many people, through the availability of abundant and cheap finance, secured for themselves an overinflated position of material wealth and its associated level of 'success'.

Large conspicuous possessions that projected an outward sense of achievement, such as luxury cars and expensive houses, were financed largely through debt. The common human traits of ambition and aspiration meant that many stretched their financial positions to dangerously high levels, to give the *impression* of success. By way of illustration, the average ratio of house prices to earnings has a long-term average (calculated over more than 40 years) of 4.1. At the peak of the speculative property bubble, in October 2007 (just before the global financial crisis), when many consumers and home owners were borrowing at unsustainable levels it reached a high of 6.39. In essence, we were trying to buy more than we could afford. [11] Whilst this financial madness (and the free and easy access to cheap debt) continued, it gave the impression that many of us were achieving rapid success. However, this success – unless it was backed by genuine achievement – was nothing more than a chimera. [12]

The second reason why a belief in rapid success persists in our thinking is because when success does manifest for an individual, in all its splendour and glory, it appears to come suddenly and often with no indication of the amount of effort that an individual has made to ensure his or her success. By way of analogy consider how water changes state. If you continue to cool it there comes a tipping point when all of a sudden it becomes ice. Likewise if you continue to heat it, a definite threshold is reached after which it rapidly transforms into steam. In my experience, there is *a tipping point for high performance and success*, when all the learning, practice and effort an individual has made accumulates and we witness a dynamic shift in performance that appears to happen all of a sudden.

Rapid success is an intoxicating myth.
Genuine success requires persistent effort.

Consider the extent to which Andre Agassi's dad pushed him in his childhood years to make the kind of effort that would eventually land him eight tennis Grand Slam titles. In his revealing autobiography - *Open* - Agassi wrote:

My father says that if I hit 2,500 balls each day, I'll hit 17,500 balls each week, and at the end of one year I'll have hit nearly one million balls. He believes in math. Numbers he say don't lie. A child who hits one million balls each year will be unbeatable.

Much of Agassi's graft was done away from public gaze and so when, in December 1988, at the age of 18, he became the quickest player in tennis history to surpass a million dollars in career prize money (playing just 43 tournaments in the process) the world looked on in amazement at this 'sudden' achievement.

The final reason why a belief in rapid success has endured is that some high achievers *hide the ladder of success* that they have climbed which makes their eventual success look all the more spectacular and mystical. Rather than attribute their success to a hard-working nature, these individuals are happy for others to believe that their success has effortlessly flowed from an innate or God-given talent. The Clinical psychologist Dr Fiona O'Doherty explains why some take the decision to hide the ladder of success:

... something happens to some successful people – they hide the ladder. By this I mean that, in the self-satisfaction of their success, they seek to be admired for their greatness and do not wish to see this "greatness" tarnished by the true picture of a thousand small steps up a shaky ladder. [13]

Given all the reasons why rapid success appears to be an achievable aim, it creates a real sense of disillusionment when we do not progress at the exceptional rate we believe is possible. And herein lies the key problem of believing that 'anything is possible in no time at all': when our unrealistic hopes fail to 'instantly' materialise we begin to severely doubt our own ability. In turn, we may look at other successful individuals and believe that they *have* achieved the rapid success that we ourselves have failed to attain. To soften our disappointment, we may begin to believe that the super-achievers – the Inspired Movers of this world – must innately possess something that we don't: a *natural talent that they were fortunate to possess at birth*. But is this a fair assumption to make?

Natural talent and the long road to mastery

When we see the effortless brilliance of an Inspired Mover gracefully displayed before us it is understandable that many of us could be led to believe that their accomplishments are due to a divine inheritance that is uniquely theirs to enjoy. The eulogising language sometimes used by the media to describe their talents further perpetuates this belief; read for example, the words one journalist wrote about the hugely talented Roger Federer:

He moves with feet that whisper when most squeak, guided by instincts more sixth sense than court sense, his head held still, as if balancing a book on top.... Federer covers the court in a way that tennis players say they cannot compare to other tennis players. They say he plays with the anticipation of Larry Bird and the graceful athleticism of Michael Jordan. The nimble feet of Jerry Rice. The timing of Wayne Gretzky. The poetic power of Muhammad Ali.[14]

Very few would argue that Federer is not an extraordinary talent; but is it fair to say he was born this way? I would say, no. As the tennis coach and former player Darren Cahill pointed out when he first saw Federer at the age of 13 or 14, he was still very much a work in progress. As Cahill described, "Roger struck me as being loose in everything. His forehand was really fast [but] he mis-hit a lot of balls... his footwork was a little bit all over the place, he was a bit lazy with his feet. You could see he had beautiful hands and good hand-eye [co-ordination]... but he didn't hit the ball square all that often." [15]

Federer, like all Inspired Movers, had to *master his craft to get to the top of the game*. As Seppli Kacovski, one of his childhood coaches, remarked, a large part of Federer's genius was perhaps his ability to learn: "The learning process went so quickly with him, and I never had to repeat anything. He had an enormous ability to grasp what I was telling him." [16]

Some might argue that Federer possessed the 'right genes' which allowed him to learn so effectively and possess such great co-ordination. As we shall discuss further in the Fifth Master – *Move with Precision* – the nature versus nurture debate is difficult to conclusively win one way or the other. However, the belief in innate talent has enjoyed the upper hand ever since Sir Francis Galton, the respected English polymath, wrote his influential book *Hereditary Genius* in 1869, in which he stated the upper limit of our performance (after taking into account any necessary training or practice) was genetically endowed for each of us. However, recent leading-edge research into the study of expert performance by the psychologist Anders Ericsson and his colleagues has shed new light on the subject of talent acquisition; it has pushed the door wide open to all of us who aspire to be better. *There is clear evidence that we can all be more and do more but there is a price to be paid for the highest levels of success.*

Ericsson's study was compiled in the early nineties and is one of the most extensive research projects ever undertaken into the causes of high performance. The main and hugely influential finding of that study is that, based on current evidence, it takes a minimum of 10 years [17] of intensive practice to achieve mastery in any complex field or task or what Ericsson refers to as "expert" or "superior reproducible performance". [18] His findings support the earlier work of two American psychologists, Herbert Simon and William Chase, who in their seminal 1973 research paper found that the best chess players needed to spend over 10 years playing the game before winning at an international level.[19]

Ericsson's study seems to dismiss the idea of rapid progression to the top and supports the old adage that "an overnight success takes about 10 years!" His findings have been supported by a wave of best-selling books on talent which reveal how the world's successful elite have all had to pay the necessary price of success – *years of intensive practice.*

Dedication is the price of success.
Mastery and talent are its rewards.

In *Outliers,* Malcolm Gladwell brought to light the tremendous amount of practice the likes of The Beatles completed before they were able to enjoy significant success – it turns out they performed 1,200 times before they enjoyed their first real success in 1964. [20] Gladwell also cited the example of Bill Gates who, by the time he had dropped out of Harvard to lay the initial foundations for Microsoft, had relentlessly been programming for seven years in a row and had surpassed *10,000 hours* of committed practice (Gladwell's alternative definition of the 10-year rule proposed by Ericsson).

In *Talent is Overrated,* Geoff Colvin revealed that even so-called "childhood prodigies" such as Mozart owed their brilliance to the prodigious amount of hard work and practice that they had completed during their childhood years. By the time Mozart composed his Piano Concerto No.9 (considered by many to be his first masterpiece), he was 21 - a relatively young age for a composer but by then he had already been practising and refining his abilities for 18 years.

In *Bounce,* Matthew Syed painted a similar picture of childhood prodigies in the world of sport; like Mozart, Tiger Woods - thanks to the efforts of his highly attentive father and countless carefully constructed training sessions - had also accrued thousands of hours of dedicated practice by his mid-teens.

All the recent evidence, therefore, on talent development and the mastery of highly skilful and complex moves that bring significant achievements, suggest unequivocally that:

- *Manifesting success requires hard work.*

- *There is no fast track to high achievement.*

- *There is no such thing as rapid or overnight success.*

Does that mean, the idea of accelerated progress, should be entirely discarded? I would say yes and no:

Yes – the idea of a short-cut to *mastery or elite performance* should be discarded.

No – the idea of short-term improvement still has some merit.

Allow me to explain. Whilst mastery of a complex profession or skill may take a decade or so of training, Ericsson and his colleagues also revealed in *The Cambridge Handbook of Expertise and Expert Performance* (their 900 page bible of performance) that most everyday skills (such as driving a car, playing chess, or 'bad' golf) are relatively easy to acquire, at least to an 'acceptable' level of performance, in less than 50 hours; [21] and so, the notion that improvement can to some extent be attained in a relatively short period of time holds true to a degree.

However, I feel strongly that it is important not to encourage the false hope that major changes or dynamic shifts in performance could be attained through short bursts of effort. Psychologists, mentors, and coaches like myself are, on occasion, able to help talented individuals enhance their performance levels by helping them attain an optimal inner state - *of thinking and feeling* - that helps them to more fully express the talent they have *already worked hard to possess.* However, attaining a higher level of skill, subtlety, or sophistication in our work can only ever be the product of time.

If we are to accomplish the First Master Move, and move progressively in order to pursue our Ideal Way Forward – *what we want to achieve* through expressing *who we choose to be* – we must take into account that *success is the triumph of persistence. Transformational change takes time.*

The everyday effort of success

It stands to reason that success takes time and great effort. In my opinion, it explains why there is a dearth of talent at the very top of each profession; the unwillingness by many people to do the necessary work to achieve the highest levels of performance is a real constraint.

In my work with large corporates, for example, there is always talk amongst senior executives about *the war for talent* or of the need to recruit (rather than develop) 'A' players. Bill Gates is famous for saying that if you took the 20 smartest people out of Microsoft it would be an insignificant company. *Inspired Movers are hard to find.* If it was easy sports stars in the NBA or NFL would not receive such huge salaries; the likes of Real Madrid would not have paid Tottenham Hotspur a reported world-record transfer fee of £85.3 million for the services of Gareth Bale. It is a simple case of supply and demand. *Talent is in big demand but in short supply.*

The rewards are therefore significant for those individuals who dare to dream and who are prepared to work tremendously hard to make that dream a manifested reality.

The high price of success makes Inspired Movers a rarity. Their hard earned talent makes them priceless.

Make no mistake about it - the very best have made a huge commitment to hard work that, in time, differentiates them from the rest. They have made sacrifices others are not prepared to make. When a prospective client asks me if it is easy to make significant changes in their career or level of performance, I always say, "No, it's really hard... but there is a way," and I then take note of their reaction.

In many cases I see their eyes glaze over and a sense of uneasiness spread across their face. They did not expect how achieving the Ideal

Way Forward in their lives would be such hard work. In some cases, however, I see something powerful happen: a fire burns brightly in their eyes, a sense of encouragement spreads across their face and they give me a look as if to say, *"I'm ready to commit. I'm ready to do whatever it takes build my success. I believe with time I can succeed."*

This last statement epitomises what it means to move with progression. It is moving forward in life with the inspired belief that *more is possible* but with the grounded and level-headed attitude that our very best accomplishments will be achieved with *time* and *effort*. The word *progression* actually hints at this important fact; the Oxford dictionary defines it as the process of developing *gradually* towards a more *advanced state*. The Ideal Way Forward for each of us grows in complexity and sophistication *over time*. As we will discover later in the Fifth Master Move – *Move with Precision* – the optimal moves that create success are perfected through a long process of refinement.

It is important therefore to not expect too much too soon. We must not follow the potentially debilitating mantra of *perfection or nothing* when we are starting out on a process of transformational change. Success is very much based on the pillars of *patient and persistent application*. As Winston Churchill said: "Every day you may make progress. Every step may be fruitful. Yet there will stretch out before you an ever-lengthening, ever-ascending, ever-improving path. You know you will never get to the end of the journey. But this, so far from discouraging, only adds to the joy and glory of the climb."

The Ideal Way Forward is mastered progressively. The small steps we make today pave the way for the optimal moves we shall unleash tomorrow.

However, the power of everyday effort does accumulate with time. Great success often flows along the lines of a story I once read.

A King once promised any gift to one of his subjects, who proceeded to ask for one grain of rice for the first square on a chess board, two for the second, four for the third, eight for the fourth, and so on, up to the 64th square of the chess board. The King was surprised by the seemingly modest request but his subject knew how the power of accumulation works – by the 64th square of the chess board he had accumulated great riches of rice (18,446,744,073,709,551,615 grains to be precise).

Concerted effort and dedicated practice have a similar effect. Their effects multiply and bring you significant success in due course. Our rewards may accumulate slowly at first but our later successes and achievements can often surpass even our most hopeful expectations – especially for those of us who move progressively, learning day by day, growing stronger month on month, and achieving success year on year.

Applying the First Master Move:

Through the First Master Move we discovered that:

- The idea that 'anything is possible in no-time at all' is an intoxicating but harmful concept.

- False hope and unrealistic timescales for change create disillusionment and doubt in our abilities which may derail our progress.

- More is possible in life but there is no fast-track to significant success.

- Inspired Movers have reached exceptional levels of success and performance through intensive practice and hard work.

- Few people are prepared to pay this price for success. For those that move progressively to pursue their Ideal Way Forward – *what they want to achieve* through expressing *who they choose to be* – the rewards are exceptionally high.

Moving with progression means proceeding forward with the inspired belief that *more is possible* but with the level-headed attitude that our very best accomplishments will be achieved through *time* and *effort*.

Now that it is clear that mastering the moves of success will take a massive amount of hard work - ask yourself, honestly, how this discovery makes you feel. Are you *encouraged* that - no matter how hard - there is a way to great success? Or do you feel *discouraged* by the price that needs to be paid for high attainment? If you are put off by the demands that will be imposed upon you - you need to question the direction in which you are hoping to go, or question whether you have sufficient motivation to make your hopes a reality.

Remember, an impatient or expedient approach to progress will only reduce or cap your ultimate level of performance. Do not be anxious or rushed in your pursuit of success. As Aesop's fable of *'The Hare and the Tortoise'* revealed, a steady and methodical approach wins out over short-lived and excitable bursts of activity. Moving with progression is a valiant task of lifelong perseverance, learning, adaptation, evolution and growth. It can be achieved by constantly asking yourself a question that the greats of every profession repeatedly ask themselves: *how can I change for the better?*

In addition to any specific training, the process of change requires us to tap into a vital resource of potential growth: the *tacit knowledge* that we acquire every day through each and every experience we have. Often we are not aware of how much valuable information we are taking in day-upon-day; hence the reason why it is called tacit knowledge - the word tacit is derived from the Latin word *tacitus* which means silent.

To make the most of our tacit knowledge we need to make it *explicit*. We need to draw it out and be conscious of it so that we can make more effective use of it. This is the source of the practical intelligence we discussed in part one of the book. The richer, more interesting and more progressive a life that you lead the greater the quality and scope of this tacit knowledge. When I work with clients one of my primary roles is to help them to tap into this deeply valuable yet silent knowledgebase that they possess within themselves.

To make tacit knowledge explicit we can undertake a powerful yet simple practice – we can spend 10 or 15 minutes *each and every night* reviewing the most important events and experiences of the day. As the great philosopher Pythagoras said, in one of his Golden Verses: *"Never suffer sleep to close thy eyes after thy going to bed, till thou has examined by thy reason all thy actions of the day. Wherein have I done amiss? What have I done? What have I omitted that I ought to have done?"* [22]

Following Pythagoras' lead, I urge you to ask yourself three questions when considering the events of each day or when reflecting back on a personal performance:

What worked? What didn't work? What do I need to change?

These three questions hold much power. They can help you to make performance gains similar to those made by the Inspired Movers you have read about in this chapter.

This daily evening review exercise serves many useful purposes; it avoids the intellectual arrogance that can flow from the belief that you know all there is to know; it helps you to refine your actions; it helps you move progressively forward each day in a better way as you continue to learn from your environment.

As we shall see in the next Master Move, *the Ideal Way Forward requires us to look ahead with purpose.* However, it is important not to lose sight of the fact that it is by *looking back* that we discover how to move forward more effectively. By consolidating our experiences of today we learn how to capitalise on the opportunities of tomorrow: *that is moving with progression.*

---

[1] Thorpe, Vanessa, *'Shelf-help' books to fill publishers' coffers in 2014,* The Observer, 28th December 2013.

[2] Byrne, R., *The Secret,* Sydney, Simon & Schuster, 2006, p175.

[3] Kahneman, D., *Thinking Fast & Slow,* London, Penguin Books, 2011, p.255

[4] http://www.ted.com/talks/jeff_han_demos_his_breakthrough_touchscreen.html

[5] See website article: http://www.marketwatch.com/story/warren-buffett-more-myth-than-legend-2013-07-03

[6] Colvin, G., *Talent is Overrated,* Boston, Nicholas Brealey, 2008, p12-13

[7] Source: Wikipedia/IAAF website: http://www.iaaf.org/news/news/2011-already-a-record-breaking-year-for-the-m

[8] Michael Johnson quoted in an interview for Laureus.com: http://www.laureus.com/news/track-legend-michael-johnson-says-usain-bolt-can-run-94-secs-100-metres

[9] Denison, J., *Bannister and beyond: The mystique of the four minute mile,* Breakaway Books, 2003.

[10] Ericsson, K.A., *The Influence of Experience and Deliberate Practise on the Development of Superior Expert Performance,* in *The Cambridge Handbook of Expertise and Expert Performance,* eds. Ericson, K.A., Charness, N., Feltovich, P.J., and Hoffman, R.R., Cambridge, Cambridge University Press, 2006.

[11]

http://www.telegraph.co.uk/finance/personalfinance/houseprices/10548795/201 3-house-price-rises-home-owners-made-1131-a-month.html..

[12] I gained a unique and first hand insight into the effect of debt on consumerism through working in the financial industry for over ten years.

[13] O'Doherty, R., *Irish Medical News,* 27 September 2010, p.44

[14] Bishop, G., *Federer Exerts His Power From The Ground Up,* 30 August 2009 New York Times.

[15] Bower, C., *Roger Federer, the greatest,* London, John Blake Publishing, 2011, p30.

[16] Bower, C., *Roger Federer, the greatest,* London, John Blake Publishing, 2011, p31.

[17] Note, as Ericsson, himself concedes - when it comes to the ten-year rule, ten is not necessarily a magical number and the amount of intense training required to become an internationally acclaimed performer differs across various professions. See the Fifth Master Move.

[18] Ericsson, K.A., *The Influence of Experience and Deliberate Practise on the Development of Superior Expert Performance,* in *The Cambridge Handbook of Expertise and Expert Performance,* eds. Ericson, K.A., Charness, N., Feltovich, P.J., and Hoffman, R.R., Cambridge, Cambridge University Press, 2006.

[19] Chase, W.G., & Simon H.A., *Perception in chess,* Cognitive Psychology, 1, p33-81

[20] Gladwell, M., *Outliers,* London, Penguin, p48-50

[21] Feltosich, P.J., Prietula, M.J., & Ericsson, K.A., *Studies of Expertise from Psychological Perspectives,* in *The Cambridge Handbook of Expertise and Expert Performance,* eds. Ericson, K.A, Charness, N., Feltovich, P.J., and Hoffman, R.R., Cambridge, Cambridge University Press, 2006.

[22] Dacier, A., & Rowe, N., *Commentary of Hierocles on the Golden Verses of Pythagoras,* London The Theosophical Publishing Society.

Master Move 2
Move with Purpose

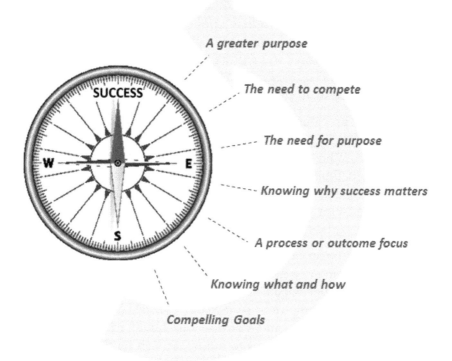

A greater purpose

The need to compete

The need for purpose

Knowing why success matters

A process or outcome focus

Knowing what and how

Compelling Goals

Inspired Movers know their Ideal Way Forward. They are guided by the path that best serves their purpose.

Why goals matter

By some miracle of nature we, as humans, are self-aware and conscious of the world around us. Psychologists have coined the term *metacognition* to describe the unique quality we possess of being able to *think about how we are thinking*. Metaphorically speaking, we can step outside ourselves and reflect upon what is going on within us and outside us. Most importantly we can look ahead and imagine the future. The vision and foresight we are blessed with means *we can choose our own Ideal Way Forward in life*. We can pursue the success that matters and interests us the most.

As we learnt previously, the Ideal Way Forward in any situation represents what we want to achieve *through* expressing who we choose to be. Who we choose to be (and the values we choose to express) is a defining element of Inspired Movement – that shapes every move we make – which we will explore in the last of the Seven Master Moves. Our focus for now is the direction of the Ideal Way Forward: *Knowing what it is that we want to achieve.*

The distinctly human quality of looking ahead, and setting ourselves goals, originates in an area of our brain known as the *prefrontal cortex,* which is more developed in humans than in other primates. Psychologists frequently refer to it as the *'executive centre'* as it allows us to intelligently direct and visualise our future moves, and hold goals long enough in our minds to follow through on them.

Goals appear to matter deeply to us. The American educator and economist George Loewenstein, suggests that the need to set and complete goals is hardwired into every one of us. [1] He made this conclusion after undertaking a study into the motivations of mountain climbers; specifically he explored why they were prepared to put up with the *miseries* of this tough pastime, such as hunger, thirst and pain. The answer, as Loewenstein discovered, is simple enough; climbing a mountain successfully – or completing any other challenging goal – generates a tangible sense of achievement that energises and enlivens us.

Succeeding in our aims appears to have a distinctly beneficial effect on our wellbeing. Research has revealed, for example, that Oscar winners live on average four years longer than Oscar nominees with all other measures being equal. [2] Moreover, this finding doesn't appear to be a peculiar quirk of Hollywood; it has also been reported that Nobel Prize winners live on average one to two years longer than colleagues who were nominated but not awarded the prize. [3] It appears that the feeling of achievement has a powerful effect on our body and mind.

To see ahead is an inner gift.
To achieve what we imagine is success.

The need to set and follow through on goals that stretch our capabilities certainly appears to sustain, captivate and enthral us. Through the course of history we have set ourselves goals that involve a great deal of effort - not to mention a great deal of pain - to accomplish; goals that have become more daring and complex over time.

On October 14th 1947, for example, Chuck Yeager became the first man in history to fly faster than the speed of sound after he was released in an experimental rocket-propelled Bell X1 jet from a B-29 bomber at an altitude of 45,000 feet. On exactly the same day 65 years later, Felix Baumgartner became the first person to break the sound barrier by *freefalling* from a hot-air balloon 23 miles up in space (an altitude of approximately 128,000 feet). [4]

Challenging goals stretch our present capabilities and future possibilities. The ability and desire we possess to conceive and achieve more complex and compelling moves in life, drives forward the progress and innovation that we explored in the last Master Move. Working in tandem, our hearts and minds allow us to dream, imagine and create a more compelling future. Should we wish to do so, we can determine our own purpose. We can set our own goals. The very best amongst us use the gift, of choosing their Ideal Way Forward in life, to powerful effect.

Knowing the Ideal Way Forward

Many people are familiar with the well-known 'Yale Goal Study' that sought to demonstrate the power of setting goals. According to some sources, in 1953 a group of researchers questioned Yale's graduates to ascertain how many of them had written down definite goals that they hoped to achieve in the future; apparently only 3% of the graduates surveyed had done this. Twenty years later researchers managed to locate the same group of Yale graduates and upon questioning them, for a second time, they discovered something astounding: *the 3% that had written down goals in 1953 had accumulated more personal financial wealth than the other 97% of the class put together.* This compelling study has been quoted and championed ever since by many self-help writers and motivational gurus who swear by its findings. There is just one problem, however; it appears to be made up! Despite it being widely quoted and cited as a classic piece of success-based research, no-one can actually produce *any evidence* that the study was ever conducted. [5]

There is, possibly, a good reason why so many writers and readers alike may have believed in the authenticity of the Yale study: broadly speaking its findings are plausible. The ability to *think ahead* and contemplate what we would like to achieve in life is more likely to improve our chances of success than not. Certainly, whenever we get a glimpse into the mindset of life's high achievers, it becomes patently clear that their success is not the product of chance or some vague hope. Nothing appears to be arbitrary about how they move. They know the Ideal Way Forward in all situations that matter to them. Everything they do is *on purpose.*

Inspired Movers have a clear idea of what they intend to achieve and they focus hard until it becomes a reality. For example when speaking about his success, the basketball star Michael Jordan once said, "I visualized where I wanted to be, what kind of player I wanted to become. I knew exactly where I wanted to go, and I focused on getting there."

Jack Nicklaus, one of the greatest golfers of all time, was equally unequivocal about what contributed to his success when he said, "I never hit a shot, even in practice without having a sharp, in focus picture of it in my head." [6]

Dennis Bergkamp, the former Arsenal and Dutch International footballer, revealed that even in the midst of a fast-paced game he had a clear idea about what he intended to do: "When I played in Holland, I always tried to lob the goalkeeper. People used to say, 'Oh, you're always only trying to make a nice goal'. But I said, 'listen, if the goalie is a little bit off his line, how much space do you have on his left or right? It's not a lot. And how much space do you have above him? There is more. It's a question of mathematics." [7]

Inspired Movers in business work in the same way. They also generate success with a clear goal in mind. Michael Dell wrote in his book, *Direct from Dell: Strategies that Revolutionized an Industry*, that at the end of 1986 he set a goal for the company to achieve $1 billion in turnover by 1992. In fact by 1992 the company was actually doing twice this amount. [8] Dell said that this success came from setting a big goal that challenged him and his organisation with the task of thinking about how it could be achieved. This thinking resulted in the company unleashing a decisive move that gave them the edge over its competitors: they gave their customers the ability to buy an ever-improving product at a consistently cost-effective price *direct* from the company.

Jack Welch, the ex-CEO of General Electric, also achieved great success by setting a clear strategy for the company that left none of his colleagues with any misconceptions about what they needed to do. Welch told every GE business that they would have to become either number one or number two in their field, or else they would be sold off. Welch's uncompromising goal for the company set in motion a wave of Inspired Movement across the organisation as each business put into play a series of competitive moves designed to give them the much coveted spot of number one or two in their industry. Welch's compelling strategy for the business worked. In 2000 (the final year of Welch's nineteen year spell as GE's CEO), the company generated an income of $12.7 billion on $130 billion of turnover. In the six years prior to that, GE had doubled its sales and attracted the accolade of "most valuable company in the world". [9]

Inspired Movers pursue a future that is clear and compelling. Their every move is on purpose.

Whether it is Michael Jordan or Jack Nicklaus or Michael Dell or Jack Welch, Inspired Movers know that it is the *unswerving pursuit of a single minded goal* that creates success. They have developed the capacity to *focus their minds* for concerted periods of time on a goal that matters deeply to them. Their ability to concentrate their will in this way makes them a *force of nature*; having the power to intentionally invest and parlay their energies in a chosen direction allows them to wield greater influence over the course of life. Their actions reflect the sentiment conveyed by William Ernest Henley in the final two lines of his poem *Invictus:*

I am the master of my fate:
I am the captain of my soul.

These two sentences, short as they are, capture a deep conviction that many of us hold in our stronger and more inspired moments; *we feel we can determine the course of our lives* or at least determine our response to life's events. Victor Frankl powerfully demonstrated this idea in his classic book *Man's Search for Meaning* which tells his personal story about the struggle for freedom and dignity in a Nazi concentration camp: a struggle which resulted in Frankl's inspiring observation that no matter how difficult or challenging life becomes - *we always have the freedom to choose our response to any situation.*

The ability to choose freely which move to make next in life is the cornerstone of Inspired Movement and all high achievement. As one Chief Executive Officer of Sony said, "The only way to be able to predict the future is to create it." The idea that we can control the way life, a situation, or a game, unfolds is central to the success of all Inspired Movers; *they master their fate by working hard* to develop the talent and skill which gives them greater control and freedom in their work. Operating at their very best they possess the ability to unleash decisive and winning moves *how they want* and *when they want*. Their journey towards this high level of mastery, however, must begin with a clear idea of *how* to pursue their compelling goal.

Inspired and Intelligent goal setting

When we think of goal setting, the acronym SMART may spring up in the minds of personal development aficionados. As it has been widely documented we are more likely to achieve success when our goals are *Specific, Measurable, Action-orientated, Realistic* and have a set *Timeframe* for accomplishment. SMART goals break down our journey to success into clearly defined and manageable steps. They provide a *process* to work to - through which we can set specific goals, that lead to specific strategies, techniques and tactics that create the success we desire. In the language of Inspired Movement, *process goals* represent the optimal moves we need to master if we wish to perform at our very best.

However, another approach to goal setting is to set ourselves a compelling *outcome* goal; this is a clear vision of the success we desire and the Ideal Way Forward we intend to achieve. Process and outcome goals represent two different goal setting strategies, but which has the upper hand when it comes to creating success?

In the late nineties, researchers interested in finding out the answer, used novice darts players to explore the effectiveness of process and outcome goal setting strategies. [10] The researchers split the players participating in their experiment into three groups. Players in the process goal group focused on rehearsing specific steps for acquiring a high quality technique such as improving the take-back, release, and follow-through phases of the dart-throwing action. Players in the outcome group, however, focused on improving their scores rather than explicitly focusing on their technique. A third group of players were taught how to *shift* their goals from process to outcome goals once a higher degree of dart throwing skill had been attained. In previous experiments, the researchers had found that process goals were more effective than outcome goals with novice dart throwers. Their new findings, however, revealed that players who *shifted* from process to outcome goals *outperformed* players who stuck solely to one type of goal strategy.

These research findings have an important bearing on our discussion of Inspired Movement: process *and* outcome goals are *equally* important. If we are to manifest Inspired Movement we need to know the Ideal Way Foreword (our outcome goal) but crucially - as the examples of Michael Jordan, Jack Nicklaus, or Jack Welch demonstrate - we also need to know the precise optimal moves (our process goals) that can achieve this Ideal Way Forward. Focusing on our Ideal Way Forward provides an inspired edge to our goal setting; focusing on the optimal moves brings a much needed intelligence and shape to the process.

Inspiration is knowing the Ideal Way Forward.
Intelligence is knowing the moves to achieve it.

Knowing *what* goals we want to achieve and *how* we can achieve them is the springboard to all success. A powerful example of this is the story of the American diver Laura Wilkinson. On the run-up to the 2000 Olympics, Wilkinson broke three toes, which prevented her from entering the water. Driven by a powerful desire to compete successfully at the Olympics, Wilkinson decided to sit on the diving platform each day for a number of hours, visualising in her mind detailed scenes of each one of her dives. Her approach paid off in a big way when she won gold for her 10 metre platform dive. [11] Visualising, and mastering the specific optimal moves required to create success, is something we will pick up in greater detail in our exploration of the Fifth Master Move – *Move with Precision.* For now, however, let us consider a third and *vital* element to successful goal setting.

In addition to knowing what we want to achieve, and knowing how we can achieve it, we also need to know *why* we want to achieve a certain goal. In other words, we need to *know* our purpose in life so that we can move *with* purpose through it. Finding our purpose is by no means an easy task.

The difficulty with purpose

Purpose is a quality whose significance we can easily miss or overlook. It may perhaps seem strange that in a world that is so busily engaged in doing 'this and that' and rushing from 'here to there' that we may live without a clear sense of purpose, or an *Ideal Way Forward* guiding our efforts. Yet there is something that I have discovered which is quite revealing. Whenever I am asked to speak before a professional or general audience I frequently ask the group of people before me a simple question:

How many of you know your purpose in life?

It is a question that nearly always throws the audience; only a smattering of people ever put their hands up to signify that they know their purpose. In my experience it seems that very few people can clearly articulate what their life is about or what their life is for.

In his poem *Leisure* William Henry Davies wrote:

What is the life if, full of care,

We have no time to stand and stare.

No time to turn at Beauty's glance,

And watch her feet, how they can dance.

If we were to take a moment to stand and stare at "Beauty's dance"- or *Nature's way* - we notice one of her most outstanding qualities; whether we observe a simple plant that turns instinctively to the sun in its search for light, or the smallest spider that weaves an intricate web to trap its prey, it is clear that nature appears to be imbued with a *deep knowing* of what it needs to do.

Generally, all the members of the animal kingdom do not deviate from their purpose of eating, reproducing, or taking basic measures to ensure their survival (such as herding together to benefit from the protection of a larger group). As ethologists would tell us, animals act with complete integrity with their purpose; much of their behaviour is governed by *fixed action patterns* that they perform repeatedly.

Contrary to nature, however, we humans appear to be riddled with doubt as to what is, or should be, our purpose in life. I concede that, for many people, contemplating their purpose is not a viable option as they are caught up in the unfortunate and desperate plight of simply surviving in the world as it is today. It is reported that a billion or so people around the world struggle to live on less than one dollar a day. [12] As Abraham Maslow pointed out in his classic work on human motivation (*Maslow's Hierarchy of Needs*) individuals who are consumed with the task of simply ensuring their basic safety, and physiological needs, will not have the time or inclination to ponder the deeper meaning of life, or how they can reach a stage of personal fulfilment - or what Maslow referred at as "*self-actualization*".

Even those of us who are employed in secure jobs that more than ensure our survival may struggle to find any time to reflect on our purpose in life as we are consumed by the pressing demands of modern-day living and the frenetic pace of our busy work schedules. We can find ourselves going from home to work and from work back to home, day in day out, without any real sense of knowing *why* we do what we do. Whilst the rest of nature happily plays out its cyclical, and predetermined, fate - we humans are prone to both boredom and fatigue which can result in our undoing.

Becoming caught in the net of habitual and unfulfilling work and life patterns can make us feel as though we share the same fate as the mythical Greek king Sisyphus who (as a result of some misdeed) was given a punishing sentence by the angry gods; for all eternity he had to push a heavy rock up a steep hill. Every time he approached the top of the hill, the rock would roll backwards to the bottom of the hill meaning the tired and dejected Sisyphus would have to begin the punishing ordeal all over again. Living the same life over and over again, or performing the same moves time after time, can dupe us into a tired, sleepy and desultory state of mind in which we exercise no active control over life. Living aimlessly in this manner not only undermines our hopes of success but can cause us to dangerously drift through life as James Allen pointed out in *As a Man Thinketh*, his classic work on self-development:

Until thought is linked with purpose there is no intelligent accomplishment. With the majority the bark of thought is allowed to "drift" upon the ocean of life. Aimlessness is a vice, and such drifting must not continue for him who would steer clear of catastrophe and destruction. They who have no central purpose in their life fall an easy prey to petty worries, fears, troubles and self-pityings, all of which are indications of weakness, which lead, just as surely as deliberately planned sins (though by a different route) to failure, unhappiness and loss...[13]

Allen's words provide a stark warning. Without purpose, there can be no real accomplishment but, more seriously, we can cast ourselves adrift on the capricious waters of life and leave ourselves open to many undesirable circumstances. We need to take control of our life if we are to avoid being washed up on the shore of failure or unhappiness.

To move aimlessly is to leave our success to chance. To chance our success is to risk and compromise our future.

Whether our thoughts are centred on surviving or succeeding in the world, we cannot afford to live aimlessly. *We need to find our purpose.* And yet despite the fact that many of us do not think about, or know of, our deeper purpose in life, huge swathes of people wake up each morning and toil hard throughout the day. We are clearly striving for something – but what exactly? If we reflect more deeply on the human condition, or on our own plight, we find that there *is*, in fact something driving much of what we do - and that is *the need to compete.*

The race to get ahead

By virtue of Darwin's pervasive theory of evolution the term "survival of the fittest" has become deeply lodged into the collective psyche of mankind. Like the rest of the animal kingdom we must compete, to a degree, to ensure our basic survival. However, where animals are content with securing their daily means of sustenance, or a partner to mate with, our need to compete goes further. Driven by the *human need for recognition* - our competition with each other takes on a wholly different level of meaning. Much of what we do is driven by *status competition* or what we euphemistically refer to as 'the rat race'. As depicted on one notorious US bumper sticker, the idea of the race is simple: "The one who dies with the most toys wins".

The result of status competition is that we can spend all our time and energy earning money so that we can buy goods that help us stand out from the crowd or, at the very least, enable us to keep up with the social elite. Thorstein Veblen, the 19th century American economist and sociologist, introduced the term "conspicuous consumption" [14] to refer to the way goods are purchased for the status they imply rather than their inherent usefulness. If status competition is our primary driver or motivation, our desire for success is simply a means to an end. We need to compete in order to amass the financial resources that are necessary to procure the very best possessions we can afford. The authors Richard Wilkinson and Kate Pickett touched on the issue of status competition in their insightful book *The Spirit Level* in which they wrote:

The problem is that second-class goods make us look like second-class people. By comparison with the rich and famous, the rest of us appear second-rate and inferior, and the bigger the differences, the more noticeable and important they become. As inequality increases status competition, we have to struggle hard to keep up. While the rich may believe their willingness to spend huge sums on a watch, a car or some other luxury item reflects their appreciation of 'attention to detail' or 'craftsmanship', what really makes the difference is what their purchases say about them relative to the rest of us. As every advertiser knows, it serves to set them apart as people of distinction - social distinction. Only the best people can have nothing but the best. [15]

As Wilkinson and Pickett touch upon, to have the best we invariably have to *become* the best. The desire to be *the* front runner in our field is powerful motivation for those of us who are driven by a need for outer recognition. It can serve as a compelling purpose which results in a deep urge to succeed. The Real Madrid and Portuguese International Footballer Cristiano Ronaldo is a good example of this. As one journalist wrote recently, Ronaldo has made it clear that his desire to be the best sits behind the tremendous application and work he puts into developing his game:

Ronaldo's whole story is one of unparalleled self-belief and personal commitment. Ever since he arrived at Old Trafford and declared his desire to become the best player in the world, he has left no stone unturned in his desire to be so. Under the tutelage of Sir Alex Ferguson (who he calls "my second dad"), he built his physique, mastered dead-ball situations, improved his heading beyond recognition, augmenting his game year-on-year. If one had to compare him to another high-sports sportsman, it might be England cricketer Kevin Pietersen. Both are mocked for their alleged vanity, but both are also obsessive in their efforts to constantly self-improve. [16]

On 13th January 2014, Ronaldo - now playing for Real Madrid - was finally awarded the much coveted FIFA Ballon d'Or which signified his status as the best player in the world for 2013. It was an award which he won for the first time in 2008 but since then it had eluded him as his main rival, Lionel Messi, had secured the prize on four successive occasions. Winning the award took a monumental effort and a sensational level of consistent skill and application on Ronaldo's behalf: in 2013 he scored at a ratio of over a goal a game and in doing so he became the quickest Real Madrid player in history to reach 200 goals for the club. [17]

Few would argue that the kind of competition that exists between great rivals such as Messi and Ronaldo doesn't serve a useful purpose. Done in the right spirit it challenges and draws the best out of us. When we are pushed hard by those competing against us we find latent qualities within ourselves that come to the fore when they are most needed. We are not consumed by this type of competition but are strengthened by it and when we engage in it we come close to the hidden meaning of the word competition which is derived from the Latin *con petire* which means "to seek together". Instead of any desire to lord it over our opponents, we find greater respect within us for true and valiant competitors who help us to perform moves of a much higher quality, and of much greater complexity, than we could do otherwise. In the grand scheme of things, Messi and Ronaldo, like all great competitors, are good for each other.

However, whilst the desire to have the best, or to be recognised as the best, is a powerful driver, status competition has its limitations and problems. For one, due to its zero sum nature (e.g. if there is a winner, by definition there must be a loser) it can lead to people making self-interested and Machiavellian moves as they get tempted to lie, cheat, deceive or find other expedient routes to the top. The use of illegal performance enhancing drugs in sport, or the irresponsible and selfish actions of some bankers and financial institutions that led to the recent global financial crisis, are poignant examples of this. There is a danger that competition and the desire for recognition can bring out the worst in us, just as much as it may bring out the best.

To be recognised as the best can create a powerful purpose, if it motivates a genuine and not an expedient effort to succeed.

There is also an increasing amount of evidence that suggests greater possessions and financial wealth (the goal of status competition) do not - beyond a certain level - bring increased happiness. For example, research conducted as far back as 1978 in the United States found that lottery winners were no more, or less, happy than those surveyed who had not won the lottery. [18] The economist Richard Layard also alludes to the problem of greater riches, with no corresponding increase in happiness, in his book *Happiness* in which he observed:

There is a paradox at the heart of our lives. Most people want more income and strive for it. Yet as Western societies have got richer, their people have become no happier. This is not an old wives' tale. It is a fact proven by many pieces of scientific research... all the evidence says that on average people are no happier today than people were fifty years ago. Yet at the same time average incomes have more than doubled. This paradox is equally true for the United States and Britain and Japan. [19]

When the desire to have the best, or to be recognised as the best, no longer sustains us we need to find a greater level of motivation. We need to look deeper within ourselves for a more compelling reason that can spur us on to new heights. In short, *we need a purpose greater and beyond just ourselves.*

A greater purpose

As mentioned at the beginning of this chapter the area of the brain known as the prefrontal cortex plays an important role in helping us set and achieve our goals. In his exceptional book *The Tell-Tale Brain,* V.S. Ramachandran (one of the world's foremost neuroscientists) provides an extraordinary insight into what happens when either the left or right lobe of the prefrontal area of the brain is damaged:

If the left prefrontal lobe is damaged, the patient may withdraw from the social world and show a marked reluctance to do anything at all... Conversely, if the right prefrontal lobe is damaged, a patient will seem euphoric even though he really won't be... Such a patient seems to lose all interest in his own future and shows no moral compunction of any kind. He may laugh at a funeral or urinate in public. The great paradox is that he seems normal in most respects: his language, his memory, and even his IQ are unaffected. Yet he has lost many of the most quintessential attributes that define human nature: ambition, empathy, foresight, a complex personality, a sense of morality, and a sense of dignity as a human being. [20]

It is interesting to note that damage to the area of the brain that shapes our ambition and interest in the future also adversely affects our sense of morality, responsible feeling, and thought, towards others. This opens up an interesting new dimension into our discussion on purpose. Traditionally, given our deep-rooted need for personal recognition, we may have believed that much of human behaviour is governed by a desire to maximise *self-interest*; yet as one research study found out - on a deeper level we may be more altruistic and less self-interested than we think.

Researchers conducted a series of experiments in which pairs of randomly selected individuals, who remained anonymous to each other at all times, played a game in which a known sum of money was given to one party (the proposer) who then divided it as he (or she) saw fit with the other party (known as the responder). Responders had the simple task of accepting or rejecting the offer. If they accepted the offer each party got to keep the share of money proposed by the proposer. If the responder rejected the offer, however, both parties got nothing.

Given the game was only played out once by each pair, it was expected that self-interested responders would accept any offer, regardless of how miserly it was, and self-interested proposers would only offer the smallest acceptable amount - sufficient to ensure the responder would accept it. Surprisingly the results showed that the average offer made was between 43 and 48 percent. [21] In other words the results suggested that there is a deep instinct within us to cooperate and share with each other, even in instances (such as those described in the research study) where the people involved never met, nor would interact with each other again.

When we cooperate we look after each other's *mutual* interests; moving beyond any personal self-interest or need for recognition we begin to try to do the best we can *for each other*; whether that is for those we love, or those that our effected by the actions we take, and the moves we make. As John Donne, the English poet, famously wrote, "No man is an Island, entire of itself; every man is a piece of the continent, a part of the main." As Donne alluded to, *we are deeply connected to each other.*

---

*None of us work or live in isolation. The moves
we make ripple out and affect each other.*

It may be no coincidence, therefore, that the part of the brain responsible for our ambition in life also has a significant bearing (as Ramachandran pointed out) on our sense of empathy. Deep down I believe we are just as much concerned with the happiness of others as we are of our own, and that by working intelligently and cooperatively together we can create an Ideal Way Forward that is beneficial for all parties concerned in any situation. As Jeremy Bentham, the 19th century English philosopher put forward, the right action in life is one that produces the greatest total sum of happiness.

In my experience of personal performance coaching, the desire to serve *a purpose greater and beyond ourselves* and to build success *with others or for others* is one of the most powerful motivational sources an individual can tap into. I believe it is more than some quaint or quixotic notion as suggested, at times, by individuals of a more selfish disposition. It represents a more enhanced and exciting Ideal Way Forward. *Working together more is possible.*

The greatest Inspired Movers are becoming increasingly alive to the fact that *cooperation leads to an enhanced level of performance and success.*

For example, the legendary basketball coach Phil Jackson revealed in his book *Sacred Hoops* how the great Michael Jordan matured over time and transformed himself from a self-interested basketball player into a *selfless multidimensional player* that worked tirelessly for the good of the team; helping his team mates in the process to secure three consecutive NBA championships. Jackson wrote that, as Jordan became older and wiser, he understood that, "it wasn't brilliant individual performances that made great teams, but the energy that's unleashed when players put their egos aside and work towards a common goal." [22]

Barcelona's magnificent 3-1 victory over Manchester United in the 2011 Champions League final is another excellent example of what happens when players can put their egos to one side and create *collective Inspired Movement.* In a game that Barcelona comprehensively dominated, they completed 662 passes to Manchester United's 301. The willingness of the Barcelona players to collectively build the play through their intricate passing philosophy was further evidenced by the number of times their *best players* were willing to give the ball to their team mates; Xavi completed 141 successful passes, Andreas Iniesta 107, and Lionel Messi (a player renowned for his skilful solo runs with the ball) completed 92 successful passes. By contrast, Manchester United's highest passer on the night was Rio Ferdinand who completed a mere 40 successful passes. [23]

Being able to put the ego, and other personal concerns, aside is something we will explore more deeply in the final Master Move –

Move with Poise, but it is worth mentioning here that the ability to go beyond self-consciousness or self-interest is something that the psychologist Mihaly Csikszentmihalyi claims can help us to more easily enter into a stronger frame of mind, and the desirable optimal state he famously describes as *flow*. Speaking of individuals who pursue a strongly directed purpose that is not self-seeking he wrote:

People who have that quality are bent on doing their best in all circumstances, yet they are not concerned primarily with advancing their own interests. Because they are intrinsically motivated in their actions, they are not easily disturbed by external threats. With enough psychic energy free to observe and analyze their surroundings objectively, they have a better chance of discovering in them new opportunities for action.[24]

Being able to move with a selfless purpose means that Inspired Movers like the Barcelona players Xavi, Iniesta and Messi, are not absorbed with bending circumstances or the play to suit themselves. Driven by Barcelona's selfless 'pass and move' philosophy they are focused on playing for the good of the team. As Csikszentmihalyi pointed out: such individuals are *intrinsically* motivated – they do what they do primarily because it feels good and for no other reason. This is a feature of deeper motivation that will become apparent when we explore the Third Master Move – *Move with Passion.*

Moving from a selfish to a more selfless purpose is also shaping the Ideal Way Forward in other areas of life. Magnanimous individuals working within the areas of scientific research, healthcare, and social entrepreneurship have typically worked with a selfless motive - but even traditional businesses that previously existed with the sole purpose of maximising shareholder wealth are looking to serve a greater purpose.

Visionary organisations and the individuals who run them are turning their attention to how their products and services can better serve life and add value to the lives of their customers. For example, in an article for the *Harvard Business Review*, the academics James Collins and Jerry Porras, outlined the core purpose, or raison d'être, of some the world's leading companies which showed that they existed for a much greater purpose than simply generating a profit.[25] HP (Hewlett Packard), for example has a desire to make technical contributions for the advancement and welfare of humanity. Wal-Mart is focused on giving ordinary folk the chance to buy the same things as rich people. Walt Disney exists to make people happy. Great businesses serve some great purpose. It is what ensures their success and customer loyalty. The fact that they exist for something important *is* important; as one recent survey pointed out young people today are three times more likely to work for a company that does something they care about. [26]

By serving a purpose greater and beyond themselves, Inspired Movers create wider possibilities for success.

Living for something greater than ourselves is becoming an increasingly powerful driver in business, sport, and all other areas of life. As we grow in maturity and wisdom we begin to seek an Ideal Way Forward that matters – *we seek a purpose that makes a difference.* When we find it, life and success take on a deeper level of meaning. We have a powerful desire to succeed because we know *why* the Ideal Way Forward we seek is so important to us. Guided by it, we begin to live with greater thought, intention and sensitivity. Holding in our minds a clear picture of the ideal life that we are striving to create, we ensure that every decision we make *serves* our purpose and that every move we make is *on* purpose.

Applying the Second Master Move:

Through the second Master Move we discovered that:

- A challenging goal stretches our present capabilities and our future possibilities.

- Inspired Movers know what they want to achieve and are single minded about achieving it.

- When it comes to goal setting, process and outcome goals are equally important. We must remain focused on the Ideal Way

Forward (outcome goals) *and* the optimal moves that will achieve it (process goals).

- Successful goal setting works on three levels: we must know *what* we want to achieve, *how* we intend to achieve it, and most importantly we must know *why* our desired success is important to us.

- Knowing *why* we do what we do reflects our deepest sense of purpose.

- Broadly speaking, our purpose may involve having the best, being the best for ourselves, or being the best we can be with or for others.

- Serving a *purpose greater and beyond ourselves* can be one of the most powerful motivational sources we can tap into.

- Through *knowing* our purpose we can move *with* purpose.

The definition for Inspired Movement I shared with you in part one of this book reveals our success in any situation rests upon our ability to perform *the optimal moves in the right place at the right time with complete alignment to the Ideal Way Forward*. The Fifth Master Move – *Move with Precision* – will cover how we can master the optimal moves that can help us achieve the Ideal Way Forward and create the success we desire. For now it is important to concentrate on the first aspect of the Ideal Way Forward; that is *what* we want to achieve and *why* it is important.

In applying the First Master Move we focused on looking back on the main events of the day through the evening review exercise. To apply the Second Master Move and to move with purpose, we need to look forward. We must imagine and see the future we want to create.

Take a few moments to first relax yourself; close your eyes, and take a few deep breaths. Then ask yourself: *What do I desire above all else in life?* Allow a picture to emerge in your mind. Focus on any specific or interesting images that form in your inner vision. Ask yourself: *What excites me about what I see? Why is achieving this goal so important to me? Who else will benefit if I create the success I desire?* This exercise is an effective way to discover your Ideal Way Forward in life.

Whenever I ask my clients to do this exercise I typically get three kinds of response:

- They can't see a vision of the future that excites or appeals to them.

- They *can* see a compelling vision of the future but they don't believe they can achieve it.

- The can see a compelling vision of the future, they believe they *can* achieve it, but they don't know how to apply themselves or move progressively enough to achieve it.

We will explore how we can enhance our level of belief or application in later chapters of the book but for now it is important that you focus on seeing your Ideal Way Forward as clearly as you can. If you are struggling to see it you may need to repeat the exercise until you can see something meaningful that excites or moves you.

Alternatively, following the advice that the late Steve Jobs gave Stanford Graduates in his famous commencement address, you may need to make sense of your life by "connecting the dots". By dots, Jobs meant the main events of your life. In his address Jobs said, "You can't connect the dots looking forward; you can only connect them looking backwards. So you have to trust that the dots will somehow connect in your future. You have to trust in something — your gut, destiny, life, karma, whatever. This approach has never let me down, and it has made all the difference in my life." [27]

To connect the dots in your own life, you can undertake the following exercise that many of my clients have found extremely useful:

- If you wrote an autobiography of your life as it is today what title would you give the book?

- What would the five main chapters of the book be called that reflect your past journey? Under each chapter heading, list 3-5 bullet points that succinctly capture the main events of each chapter.

- If you were to write the next chapter in your autobiography about what your ideal future would be like - five to ten years from now - what would it include?

- This exercise is a powerful method of finding your Ideal Way Forward; it helps you to clearly see the path behind and ahead of you. Research suggests it is a particularly effective exercise as writing about the main events of your life can help you to better understand and find deeper meaning in them. [28]

When seeking your purpose in life it is important to remember how prone to doubt we can be as human beings. Given that we learned from the First Master Move that becoming a success involves making a concerted effort over a prolonged period of time, it is natural to question if we are on the right track given the heavy investment of time and energy it involves. It is not surprising therefore that, when talking to my clients or to delegates at an event where I have been invited to speak, one question I regularly get asked is:

How will I know if I've found my purpose or my Ideal Way Forward in life?

My answer is simple. As we will discuss in the next Master Move, when you discover your true purpose, it will command your whole attention. It will compel you into action. It will captivate your heart and mind so that you desire to do nothing else other than to answer its calling. As one old quote says, "If God should commission two angels, one to sweep a street and the other to rule an empire, they could not be induced to exchange their calling."

Discovering your purpose will have a significant bearing on your life. Moving with this purpose in mind will light up the road before you. When you see your Ideal Way Forward you will feel a palpable sense of excitement. As this excitement grows it will transform into a *passion* that burns within you. As we will discover in the next Master Move, when your *passion connects with your purpose* you will tap into an irrepressible energy that spurs you on to a greater level of success.

[1] Loewenstein, G., *"Because It Is There: The Challenge of Mountaineering...for Utility Theory,"* Kyklos 53, no.3, 1999, p315-343

[2] Redelemeier, D.A., & Singh S.M., *Annals of Internal Medicine,* 145, 2006. P.392

[3] Rablen, M.D., & Oswald, A.J., *Journal of Health Economics,* 27, 2008, pp.1462-1471

[4] See online CNN article, *Chuck Yeager retraces history in the sky, breaking the sound barrier – again,* October 15th 2012 - http://edition.cnn.com/2012/10/15/us/nevada-yeager-anniversary-flight/

[5] http://www.fastcompany.com/27953/if-your-goal-success-dont-consult-these-gurus

[6] Nicklaus, J., and Boden K., *Golf My Way,* New York, Simon & Schuster, 1974 p.79

[7] - See more at: http://www.theclockend.com/featured/top-10-dennis-bergkamp-quotes#sthash.Fk9Lm4hy.dpuf

[8] Dell, M., with Freedman, C., *Direct from Dell: Strategies that Revolutionized an Industry,* London, Harper Business, 1999.

[9] Welch, J., with Byrne, J., *Jack: What I've learned Leading a Great Company and Great People,* London, Headline.

[10] Zimmerman, B.J., & Kitsantas, A., *Development phases in self-regulation: Shifting from process to outcome goals,* Journal of Educational Psychology, 89, 29-36, 1997.

[11] Loehr J., & Schwartz T., *The Making of a Corporate Athlete,* Harvard Business Review, January 2001, 120-128.

[12] Collier, P., *The Bottom Billion: Why The Poorest Countries Are Failing and What Can Be Done About It,* Oxford, 2007

[13] Allen, J., *As a Man Thinketh,* San Diego, The Book Tree, 2007 (first published in 1902).

[14] Veblen, T., *The Theory of the Leisure Class,* Oxford, Oxford University Press, 2007.

[15] Wilkinson, R., & Pickett, K., *The Spirit Level - Why Equality is Better for Everyone,* London, Penguin Books, 2010, p227.

[16] See article appearing on BBC Sport online by journalist Andy Brassell on the 12th January 2014: http://www.bbc.co.uk/sport/0/football/25675473

[17] See http://www.theguardian.com/football/2014/jan/13/cristiano-ronaldo-ballon-dor-winner-real-madrid

[18] Brickman, D., Coates, D., & Janoff-Bulman, R., *Lottery Winners and Accident Victims: Is Happiness Relative?* Journal of Personality and Social Psychology, 36, 1978, pp 917-27

[19] Layard, R., *Happiness,* London, Penguin Books, 2006, p3

[20] Ramachandran, V.S., *The Tell-Tale Brain,* London, Windmill Books, 2011, p34.

[21] Henrich, J., Boyd, R., Bowles, S., Camerer, C.F., Fehr, E., Gintis, H., & McElreath, R., *Overview and Synthesis,* in Foundations of Human Sociality, Oxford, Oxford University Press, 2004.
[22] Jackson, P., *Sacred Hoops,* New York, Hyperion 1995 p21.
[23] See : http://www.theguardian.com/news/datablog/2011/may/30/champions-league-final-data#data
[24] Csikszentmihalyi, M., *Flow*, London, Rider, p 92.
[25] Collins, J.C., & Porras, J.I., *Building Your Company's Vision,* (1996) article featured in *HBR's 10 Must Reads: On Strategy,* Boston, Harvard Business Press, 2011.
[26] Survey statistic cited in the book *Grow* by Jim Stengel, London, Virgin Books, 2012 p295.
[27] To read the transcript of Steve Job's Stanford Commencement address see: http://news.stanford.edu/news/2005/june15/jobs-061505.html
[28] Niederhoffer, K., & Pennebaker, J., *Sharing One's Own Story: On the Benefits of Writing or Talking About Emotional Experience,* In Snyder, C.R, and Lopez, J.S, *Handbook of Positive Psychology,* New York: Oxford University Press, 2002.

Master Move 3
Move with Passion

The desire to know more

Our ruling passion

Competing temptations

Dopamine-induced highs

Intrinsic motivation

The love of what we do

A story of passion

Inspired Movers excel through doing what they do best and what they most enjoy. They further their purpose by pursuing their ruling passion.

The power of passion

How will you know if you have found your Ideal Way Forward? It is the question that ended our discussion on the Second Master Move and it is the one that carries us forward now in our exploration of the Third Master Move.

As I alluded to previously, something *unmistakable* happens when you discover your Ideal Way Forward. The vision you see, or sense of it, begins to stir your heart into action. There is a powerful and positive emotional reaction to the thoughts you have entertained in your mind about your future. There begins to well up, inside you, a desire and deep feeling to outwardly achieve what you inwardly long to be, or do. This Ideal Way Forward sets alight the fuse that fires your passion and enthusiasm to follow this direction.

The Ideal Way Forward awakens a deep urge to follow its path. Passion and desire will powerfully propel us in its direction.

As the story that follows reveals, the Ideal Way Forward in time shows itself to be the right road for you; even though at the beginning of your journey, you may not sense where this road will lead or take you.

Three or four years before the publication of this book a friend of mine who knew of my desire to write a book about success, handed me an article that he had cut out of a newspaper; it was about the journey of a man that I hadn't come across before.

"Read this," he said. "You've *got* to meet this guy!"

I quickly scanned through the article; it made for fascinating reading. However, other than using the man's story as a topic for a couple of talks which I gave around that time, I thought nothing more of it until the summer of 2013. It was then, by complete coincidence, that I was introduced to the man featured in the article by one of my clients. In the months that followed he became someone whose story and character I grew to know well. The man in question was Terry Byrne and his story is one that captures the essence of the Third Master Move – *moving with passion.*

As a young man Byrne wanted nothing more than to be a footballer. Unfortunately, despite being a youth team player on the books of the English Football League club Leyton Orient F.C., he was unable to make the grade and found himself, instead, making a living as a London cab driver. Deep down, however, he knew his *passion* was for football and he felt his Ideal Way Forward lay in that direction; as Byrne told me at one of our meetings, "I loved football. I wanted to be a part of it. If I couldn't be a footballer then I wanted the next best thing - a job *in* football."

One day Byrne was in the stands of Stamford Bridge watching Chelsea F.C., a team he had supported since a boy, when he saw a job advertised in the match day programme by the team's physiotherapist: Chelsea needed a part-time sports masseur. Despite having no previous experience Byrne *saw his opportunity* and applied for the job. At the time Byrne's mother worked as an aromatherapist and hairdresser and knew how to do massage. He asked her to show him the basics but she warned him that you couldn't just learn how to massage overnight.

"I managed to get an interview however," he said with a smile. "They told me they liked my enthusiasm but they couldn't give me the job as I had no relevant qualifications. So they told me if I was serious I needed to do an appropriate course and then apply again."

Encouraged by the advice, Byrne decided to take a one-year course at the London School of Sports Massage. It was a decision that would change the course of his life. After gaining the qualification Byrne re-applied and managed to secure a role as a part-time masseur at the club. In return for his efforts he received two match day tickets each week as well as some additional taxi work from the club. Byrne, however, was undeterred by his level of remuneration (or lack of it). "I decided to be the best I could be at it," he said, "I wanted the players to really notice the difference in the treatments I gave."

The players did and when Glenn Hoddle became the Chelsea manager in 1993 and told Ken Bates, the chairman of the club at the time, that he wanted a full-time sports masseur, Byrne was awarded the job and became the first full-time sports masseur in English Football. There was just one catch however; Bates was looking to cut costs and would not pay for the salaries of both a full-time masseur and a kit man for the team. In order to secure his full-time employment at the club and pursue his dream of a job in football Byrne took it upon himself to do both jobs for an annual salary of only £15,000. Thereafter, he fully committed himself to both roles and found himself, for a time, working 18 hour days. However, the growing demands of each job made it difficult to continue with both. Byrne had to make a choice between the two jobs. On the advice of Glenn Hoddle he decided to commit himself to the field of physiotherapy and duly completed the English Football Association's two year sports injury diploma. It was a prescient move on Byrne's behalf. In 1996 Hoddle became the England Manager and subsequently offered Byrne a position within the England medical team which Byrne took up in addition to his Chelsea role.

It was in the England setup that Byrne's path crossed, for the first time, with that of a young David Beckham. The two quickly realised they had much in common. They were both from London, both their mothers were hairdressers, and both their fathers were from similar working class backgrounds. Given their like-minded upbringing, Beckham and Byrne became close friends and so when Beckham was infamously sent off for kicking out at the Argentinean defender Diego Simeone in the World Cup of France 1998 (a game which saw England lose and go home from the tournament) it was natural that Hoddle should ask Byrne to console him. As the teary-eyed Beckham walked off the pitch, it was Byrne that put his arm around him as the two made their way down the tunnel.

In the years that followed the relationship between the two grew stronger as did both their respective careers; by the time Beckham joined Real Madrid from Manchester United in 2003, Byrne had himself risen up the football ladder and had become the Director of Football at Watford F.C. It was then that Beckham asked Byrne if he'd consider moving to Spain to become his personal manager. Byrne agreed to do so and ended up managing Beckham for five years; it was an experience he *loved*.

"It was an amazing time," he told me reminiscing about that period of his life. "Just imagine working with your best mate every day and going to training and watching Zidane, Ronaldo, Roberto Carlos and Luis Figo - for a man who loves football, this was an extremely rewarding and unique experience."

In 2007, Beckham moved to Los Angeles Galaxy, a move which Byrne helped to arrange and negotiate on Beckham's behalf. However, following the birth of his son, Byrne knew the time had come for him to step away and pursue another opportunity – one, in fact, that forms a major component of the successful business he heads up today. Byrne's company *1966* manages the commercial and charitable interests of the England Football Team. Additionally he is also the Executive Vice President of Legends 10, a company which manages the commercial and intellectual property rights of Pelé - arguably the greatest footballer of all time and someone who Byrne is proud to know personally as a friend.

Byrne's story is fascinating on many levels but there is one consistent theme that resounds through it, and that is his *love of football*. It is his deep affection for the beautiful game that saw Byrne rise from being a cab driver, to a part-time sports masseur at Chelsea, to a man who has subsequently come to know and befriend some of the most respected figures within the game. But more important than this, it is his love for football that has led to Byrne having such a distinguished career in the game *in his own right*.

If Terry Byrne could give you one piece of defining career advice it would undoubtedly be: *do or be that which you love*. It is advice that has been echoed many times by other Inspired Movers and directed to all of us who harbour earnest aspirations to succeed. For example, the Oscar award winning actor Robert De Niro recently told aspiring young actors, "I always say – you've got to really love what you do. Don't expect to be famous – do it because you really love doing it and have fun doing it. I've always said if I can make a living at it, I'm happy." [1]

The current Formula One world champion, Sebastian Vettel also alluded to the importance of loving what you do in an interview he gave after winning his fourth F1 title. As Vettel told journalists, "To be that successful, of course it makes me proud, but every race and season is a new challenge. I am not lacking motivation. I'm ambitious and I want to win, and if there is a chance to win I want to take it. One of the secrets, and for the whole team, is to be in the moment. We love motor racing and we enjoy racing, so we don't need any (extra) motivation." [2]

The love of what we do takes us further.
It provides an inner drive that needs
little outer motivation.

Whether it is the driving force behind Byrne's journey in football, De Niro's award winning success as an actor, or Vettel's unquenched desire for more F1 titles, to love what you do is of huge importance. But what makes it *so* important? After all someone with as illustrious a career as Andre Agassi achieved considerable success in tennis without loving what he did. In fact, as he revealed in his autobiography, he surprisingly: "…hated it with a dark and secret passion." [3] We will return to Agassi's story later but for now let's delve into why loving what you do makes such a big difference.

The loving difference

In the influential book *The Human Side of Enterprise* the author and academic, Douglas McGregor, put forward his two theories of motivation: *Theory X* and *Theory Y*. Broadly speaking Theory X describes people who naturally dislike work and wish to do as little as possible of it. As such, Theory X individuals have to be coerced into doing work through close performance management and through being incentivised by appropriate *extrinsic* rewards such as a sufficiently high salary, bonus, or other perks which compensate them for doing work which is otherwise unrewarding and unfulfilling.

Theory Y individuals are different. They are *intrinsically* motivated and see work as inherently enjoyable; it is something that gives them the opportunity to express themselves and make use of their intelligence, imagination, and creativity.

Whether it is possible to entirely categorise each of us as Theory X or Theory Y, research suggests that individuals who do possess a happy disposition towards their work *achieve a greater level of success*. In other words happiness doesn't just flow as a result of achieving success; it can also be the *cause* of it. This was the finding of the psychologists Sonja Lyubomirsky, Laura King, and Ed Diener, who undertook an extensive exercise that reviewed hundreds of academic studies on success. [4] In their research they presented numerous accounts showing how *"positive affect"* (the term they use to describe a state of happiness and wellbeing) leads to greater success. Amongst other findings, these separate research studies showed a clear link between happiness and performance in a variety of professions. For example, they revealed:

- Happier cricket players have higher batting averages.

- Optimistic life insurance agents sell more insurance.

- Optimistic CEOs receive higher performance ratings from the chairpersons of their boards and run businesses that enjoy greater returns on investment.

- In general, happy individuals secure 'better' jobs that have more autonomy, meaning, and variety.

Happiness clearly has a big bearing on success and an individual's level of performance. A major component of this happiness is discovering the work or vocation in life that gives us a sense of intrinsic joy.

When we do something we love we become totally immersed in whatever it is. Psychologists have used the term *autotelic* [5] to describe the experience; a word derived from the Greek language which means something that is an end in itself. When an activity becomes autotelic we do it because we find it *inherently rewarding*. We become *intrinsically* rather than *extrinsically* motivated. When we are in this high and good-feeling state, the need to engage in status competition, or the need to gain recognition for our work begins to fall away which may explain why De Niro counsels young actors to not enter the profession for the fame but for the love of what they do.

When we are intrinsically motivated our work becomes more than a means to an end; we find that we are *inwardly driven* to put our heart and soul into what we do regardless of any rewards we may receive for doing it.

When our work is inherently rewarding we free ourselves from thoughts of reward and recognition and we can fully immerse ourselves in what it is that we love to do.

As Terry Byrne's story so aptly illustrates, intrinsic motivation is an incredibly powerful component of Inspired Movement. Byrne was able to put aside any personal concerns about himself such as the level of money he would earn, or the amount of recognition he would gain. He made a commitment instead to work in the game he loved. Simultaneously, he made a significant investment in himself to ensure that whatever he was asked, or required, to do was done to an exceptional standard - his every move in football therefore was of a high order. Finally he demonstrated one of the hallmark features of intrinsic motivation; by doing the work he loved he found a capability within himself to commit to the long hours of tireless work that are so necessary to achieving success.

Happy to pay the price?

The drive and determination of Inspired Movers to persevere with their work, when less motivated individuals find themselves running out of passion and commitment, is something that Lyubomirsky and her colleagues also picked up on in their research; as they observed - happy and satisfied workers are more likely to be high performers in their roles because they are less likely to exhibit "job withdrawal". [6] They have the ability to *stick* with what they do. Their love for their work literally *binds* them to the Ideal Way Forward and compels them to pursue its direction.

As we have already discovered in this book the ability to unleash the highest levels of Inspired Movement requires mastery – a mastery that typically takes 10,000 hours or ten years of committed practice. We often look on with a mixture of awe and bewilderment at those committed individuals who are willing to make such a huge sacrifice and suffer such an exhaustive amount of work in order to succeed. As the author Orison Swett Marden pointed out, as far back as 1894, "Success is the child of drudgery and perseverance. It cannot be coaxed or bribed; pay the price and it is yours." [7]

It is a price that Inspired Movers *are* willing to pay. However, whilst the quest for progression undoubtedly requires the endless repetition of the skills and abilities we hope to perfect, this work does not appear to be drudgery to those that have a high level of intrinsic drive. In his book, *Bounce*, Matthew Syed made reference to the mindset of some top sports professionals who have been able to commit themselves to hours and hours of practice since the beginning of their childhoods. Syed wrote:

But where the motivation is internalized, children tend to regard practice not as gruelling but as fun. Here is Monica Seles, the tennis prodigy: 'I just love to practice and drill and all that stuff.' Here is Serena Williams: 'It felt like a blessing to practice because we had so much fun.' Here is Tiger Woods: 'My dad never asked me to play golf. I asked him. It's the child's desire to play that matters, not the parent's desire to have the child play.' [8]

As Seles, Williams, and Woods point out, doing what we love furnishes us with a deep enjoyment to pursue our passion.

The love of what we do binds us to our work.
It sustains our interest and furthers our success.

But what exactly gives rise to this persistent inner drive? The answer lies deep in the middle of the human brain in a structure called the *striatum* which is a key component of what neuroscientists refer to as the reward network; a part of the motivation framework of the brain that makes us feel good when we do things that we enjoy. Through the use of functional magnetic resonance imaging (fMRI) machines, neuroscientists have discovered a way of peering into the brain and observing it whilst it works. These fMRI scans have shown that a major component of this reward network is the chemical messenger dopamine; the pleasure we feel when we do something we love is a result of dopamine being released in the reward network [9] which provides us with a sense of euphoria. This dopamine-induced high makes us feel deeply alive and fully engaged in the moment - something which, in turn, enhances our memory, attention and problem solving capabilities. The feel-good sensation that results from doing what we love or enjoy provides the inner drive or intrinsic motivation to *repeat the same experience* as the brain craves another dopamine fix.

If we could peer into the brain of a Seles, Williams, or Woods when they are in a state of flow and completely absorbed in their respective sports, we would see how the dopamine released in the reward network surges into the various neural circuits of their brains (that are responsible for conceiving and executing the highly skilled moves they make), strengthening them in the process and making them more likely to fire and wire together in the future. [10] (As we shall discover later in the book, the repeated *firing and wiring* [11] of neurons make our moves more efficient and effortless; it is therefore a key feature of high performance). Doing what we love, therefore, and the dopamine high that it produces, has a powerful intoxicating effect on the brain. We are *compelled* by nature to do more of what we love.

Without this intrinsic drive, however, our plight becomes altogether different. The journey to success can instead feel like a 'hard slog' and the price to be paid for this success may be too much for those of us without a genuine enthusiasm for what we do.

In my experience, when the mind is not happily absorbed in what it is doing, or is not actively employed with positive ideas, there is a danger that we can more easily succumb to negative states of mind. In such cases, the joy of performing or training can instead give way to a strong disliking of it, as Barry Cowan a former British tennis player poignantly pointed out when he said:

But it becomes more than a job, it takes over your life. If you're at the top of tennis, you're on tour 30-plus weeks of the year – and when you're doing that, everything revolves around tennis. Every decision you make, tennis is at the back of your mind. That's the main reason for burnout among tennis players in their 20s. I know this for myself – it's something you've done since you were six years old, and there's a sense that if you stop giving 100% you are doomed to failure, and that is unacceptable. No wonder so many players hate their sport – the surprise is that so few admit it. [12]

Cowan's comments highlight something I come across all too regularly through my work. Many professionals, especially those working in high profile jobs in business, sport or entertainment, discover that their minds are consumed by a fear of failure or criticism rather than being absorbed in a love of what they do. As we shall pick up on, in a later discussion in the book, these individuals become *survival orientated* rather than *success orientated*. This subtle shift in the orientation of their minds has very real consequences on their level of performance. For example, as one seasoned professional footballer revealed to me, many players do not want to have the ball for too long in competitive games (especially matches with much riding on them) in case they squander possession and have to face a negative backlash from the crowd or suffer stinging criticism from their team mates. On a similar note I have come across a number of creative performers that feel physically sick before going out on stage; performing in public can leave us with a gut wrenching feeling of being *exposed* if we slip up or 'screw up'.

When we are not absorbed by a love of what we are doing, our minds may drift to the debilitating fears of criticism and failure.

The ability to deal with the fear of failure is something we will take up further in our exploration of the Fourth Master Move – *Move with Presence* – and the ability to perform without the debilitating effects of fear is a key part of our discussion on the Seventh Master Move – *Move with Poise;* but for now it is clear that *falling out of love* with our work can cause us to withdraw or deviate from our Ideal Way Forward. We can become unsure of our next move and can begin to question the direction our lives are heading in. As the next section of this chapter reveals, we can also find ourselves open to all sorts of competing passions and alluring temptations that can reel us in with the promise of making us feel good.

Temptations on the path to success

It is at this point that Andre Agassi re-enters our discussion. From a young age it was clear that he was exceptionally gifted as a tennis player but, as he so openly shared in his autobiography, it was also a sport he despised, in part due to his father forcing him to spend hour after hour of his childhood on court practicing. Agassi wrote:

*Hit harder, my father yells. Hit **harder**. Now backhands. **Backhands.** My arm feels like it's going to fall off. I want to ask, How much longer, Pops? But I don't ask. I do as I'm told. I hit as hard as I can, then slightly harder. On one swing I surprise myself by how hard I hit, how cleanly. Though I hate tennis, I like the feeling of hitting a ball dead perfect. It's the only peace. When I do something perfect, I enjoy a split second of sanity and calm.* [13]

Agassi's words are revealing and slightly paradoxical. On some level he may have derived a certain amount of intrinsic enjoyment from tennis but driven hard by his father's vicarious dream of him becoming the world's number one tennis player, Agassi instead grew to hate the sport and at one low point in his career he succumbed to the temptation of taking the drug crystal meth. In his autobiography Agassi vividly described the effect it had on him. He said there was a moment of regret, followed by vast sadness but then came a tidal wave of euphoria that dispelled every negative thought in his mind. The "tidal wave of euphoria" sounds similar to the effect of dopamine and with good reason. As neuroscientists point out, drugs such as methamphetamine (crystal meth), cocaine, or heroin can hijack the brain's natural dopamine reward system and play havoc with its normal functioning resulting in dangerously addictive behaviours. When the reward system is overrun by these harmful substances it creates an insidious cycle of tolerance which results in a need to consume greater and greater amounts of these drugs to achieve the same high. [14] This can result in tragic consequences; in the last few years alone, a combination of alleged drug and alcohol addiction has resulted in the world losing the exceptional talents of (amongst others) the Hollywood actors Heath Ledger, and Philip Seymour Hoffman, the Glee star Cory Monteith, as well as the singer Whitney Houston.

However, whilst drugs represent a more extreme temptation, there are others of a softer kind that can also lead us astray from pursuing our passion. As it happens, doing what we love is not the only way to trigger the dopamine reward system. It also fires when we engage in activities that are essential to our survival such as eating, drinking and having sex. [15] The fact that nature has, for good reason, made these activities highly enjoyable (to ensure, at the very least, that we maintain ourselves and pass on our genes) means they can result in powerful biological urges or temptations that can be hard to resist - especially for those with a penchant for sensual or sentient experiences. The result is that they can temporarily dominate our thoughts and lead us to think of nothing else but the object of our desire.

Research compiled by psychologists at Radboud University in The Netherlands showed that men who spent even a few minutes in the presence of an attractive woman performed less well in tests designed to measure brain function than those who spent time in the company of someone they do not find attractive. One possible explanation put forward by psychologists to explain the temporary impairment in a man's cognitive functioning, when in the presence of an attractive woman, is that his thinking can become "reproductively focused". [16] Or in more colloquial terms we could say it's hard to think when we've got nothing but sex on the mind!

Whether it is sex, enticing foods, alcohol or some other mind-altering substance, every Inspired Mover has, at some stage, to choose between doing things that give a sense of short term pleasure (an instant dopamine fix) or having the self-discipline to work towards a longer term goal that will, over time, provide a bigger reward or a greater sense of achievement. This exact conundrum was the subject of one of the best-known psychology experiments of all time: *the "marshmallow test"*. The ingenious test was conceived by the psychologist Walter Mischel and involved giving four-year old children a tempting dilemma; one by one they were placed in a room containing either a marshmallow or a cookie and were told they could either eat the treat right away or alternatively they could wait 15 minutes and have the larger reward of either two cookies or two marshmallows. It turned out that approximately half the children managed to resist the temptation by focusing their attention away from the treat. The really interesting insight to this experiment, however, was what transpired ten to fifteen years later when the abilities of these very same children were examined again. The results showed a significant gap in abilities had opened up between the group that had resisted temptation and the group that had not. The 'resisters' had, in time, developed a more effective ability to focus their attention; they were less likely to take drugs; and they had substantially higher scores on intelligence tests. [17]

The findings of the marshmallow test are clear. The ability to resist temptation and instead focus our full physical, emotional and intellectual resources on our longer-term aspirations is an essential feature of success. As many of us who have reneged on New Year's resolutions, or other well intentioned plans, will know, this is by no means an easy undertaking. *Temptations are by their very nature tempting!* However, it is a feat that has been accomplished by many committed and persevering high achievers. As we have seen through the many examples already shared in this book, Inspired Movers develop an ability to keep their minds focused on their Ideal Way Forward. But how do they find a way of resisting temptation where others struggle?

If we examine one of the classic tales of resisting temptation we may believe the ability of Inspired Movers to resist temptation is one of *forced* self-control; it is the story of the mythical Greek hero Odysseus who, along with his crew, had to devise a way of resisting the irresistible but potentially fatal song of the Sirens. Sailors who became enchanted by their seductive song were lured onto the desolate island where the Sirens lived and would be condemned, by their fate, to remain and die there. As Odysseus and his fellow sailors approached the sea waters inhabited by the Sirens, he ordered his crew to fill their ears with wax so they would not hear the seductive song. He also told his men to tie him tightly to the ship's mast so that he could hear the song but instructed his men to not release him from his fetters no matter how much he begged to be set free - when enthralled by the Sirens' sweet voices.

Despite Odysseus's success at resisting the Sirens, his rigid way of overcoming temptation through physical restraint, may not be the most effective strategy; although it may help us to gain momentum at the start of any new endeavour that requires us to focus.

It is the children who were successful in resisting the temptations of the marshmallow test that perhaps provide us with the biggest clue as to how temptation can be overcome: *we need to turn our attention away from it and focus elsewhere.*

This capability is strengthened (as is our ability to navigate around any potentially derailing temptations) when we turn our whole attention to what I refer to as our *ruling passion.*

The ruling passion that furthers your purpose

Our ruling passion is that which *we are best at,* and that which *we most enjoy.* I refer to it as a *ruling* passion because when we find it, and become absorbed in it, all other desires or passions naturally become subordinated. We are able then to temper our indulgence in short-term pleasures and able to reduce the number of competing desires we entertain.

When our ruling passion captivates our attention, we naturally turn away from competing desires and temptations.

When our ruling passion takes centre stage in our lives, the high level of intrinsic enjoyment it brings us naturally begins to govern how we spend our time and energy. Given how it represents both the height of our talent and the height of our enjoyment, our ruling passion provides our greatest means of self-expression along with our deepest means of personal fulfilment; especially when we are able to make the richly rewarding move of *uniting our passion with our purpose*. As Aristotle pointed out, "Where your talents meet the needs of the world, therein lies your purpose."

When we can find the work or vocation in life that we most enjoy, that we are best at, and crucially one that allows us to fulfil the purpose that matters most to us, we then wish to do nothing more than follow the Ideal Way Forward. By definition the ruling passion then becomes the *optimal* means by which we can create success and simultaneously make the biggest contribution to the lives of others. As illustrated in Figure 3.1 when we are able to do this we move towards becoming Inspired Movers rather than what I refer to as *Impulsive Movers*. Moving with the *twin motivation* of purpose and passion our minds become polarised by greater alignment and appreciation of the Ideal Way Forward. In contrast to the short-term and weak-willed nature of Impulsive Movers, our thoughts become focused on developing our ruling passion; there are fewer competing desires in our minds and we find we are less tempted by basic instinctive urges.

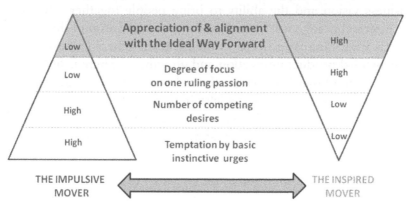

The Inspired Mover versus the Impulsive Mover

THE IMPULSIVE MOVER		THE INSPIRED MOVER
Low	Appreciation of & alignment with the Ideal Way Forward	High
Low	Degree of focus on one ruling passion	High
High	Number of competing desires	Low
High	Temptation by basic instinctive urges	Low

Figure 3.1

Very often, when working with my clients, I find that when an individual is successful in connecting their purpose with their ruling passion (and in the process achieving greater *integration* between their head and their heart) the need for recognition no longer becomes their primary driver. Instead another quintessential human instinct takes over, causing us to delve deeper and deeper into our ruling passion: it is the instinct we possess to *know more.*

The passion to know more

We humans appear to be deeply curious. The search engine Google knows this well. In a bid to satisfy our immediate curiosity Google reports that there are more than a billion Google searches done each day; an active user searches on average 25 times per day; and 15% of these daily searches are typically new searches. [18] It appears we want to know more and learn more, *especially* the Inspired Movers amongst us.

Take Satya Nadella - the new CEO of Microsoft - for example. Nadella, a long term Microsoft employee, was appointed after the company shortlisted and interviewed some of the world's best executives for the job. Upon Nadella's appointment, Bill Gates the legendary founder of the company said, "During this time of transformation, there is no better person to lead Microsoft than Satya

Nadella. Satya is a proven leader with hardcore engineering skills, business vision and the ability to bring people together. His vision for how technology will be used and experienced around the world is exactly what Microsoft needs as the company enters its next chapter of expanded product innovation and growth." [19] There is little doubt in Gates' mind that Nadella has the right credentials for the role. But what quality do you think Nadella himself feels sets him apart? In one of the first emails he sent to Microsoft employees, Nadella revealed the personal attribute that most defines him is *his curiosity and thirst for learning.*

The intrinsic desire to know more, or to go deeper and further into our ruling passion, has a significant and positive influence on another key factor of success and that is *creativity.* It is the reason why forward-thinking companies such as Google and 3M, allow their employees to spend around 10 to 20 percent of their time on any project that holds special or personal interest to them. Such projects may not always benefit these companies directly but as Geoff Colvin, Fortune's Senior Editor at Large suggests, these "follow-your-heart" projects create a culture of trust and creativity in the organisations that encourage them, giving these companies a distinct competitive advantage over their less innovative rivals. [20]

The desire to keep on learning about our ruling passion is the ultimate follow-our-heart strategy; it is what helps Inspired Movers to consistently find new levels of performance. Sebastian Vettel is a perfect example of this. We know from his quote earlier that his love for motorsport provides all the motivation he needs to win more titles. He is prepared to do what it takes to stay on top; a big part of this is the willingness to learn all the time. It is something Adrian Newey, the Red Bull car designer, says Vettel shares with past Formula One greats. Newey himself knows what it takes to succeed. In his highly successful career he has been an instrumental part of three separate title winning teams (Williams, McLaren and Red Bull). He has also had the opportunity to work up close with great Formula One champions such as Alain Prost and Ayrton Senna. Speaking of Vettel, Newey observed:

The great drivers that I have been lucky enough to work with, the thing they do all share in common is that they have that ability to drive and process at the same time. You see it with Sebastian all the time. I always have the impression that every time he gets in the car, he gets in with a bit more knowledge than he got out last time. His driving has gone from very talented but slightly raw at times to incredibly well-rounded now... It's difficult to see a chink in his armour really. He learns all the time. [21]

Vettel's desire to go further is something other high achievers know well; as the Oscar winning actress Geena Davis revealed when speaking about her secret passion for *archery* (a sport she actively pursued in addition to her acting, coming close to Olympic standard in the process) there is a compelling desire to know how good you can become. Davis, who trained five hours a day, six days a week, shooting 300 arrows a day, said:

I guess I just got hooked. It's really fun to try to see how good you can get, and I don't know how good that is. I haven't maxed out. I haven't peaked. I'm trying to get better. The last movie I made, I had them set up a target on an empty stage and I shot arrows between movie shots. [22]

Vettel and Davis both know how the positive feelings that flow from pursuing our passion help us to discover new levels of experience, knowledge and attainment. As the psychologist Barbara Fredrickson pointed out with her *Broaden and Build Theory of Positive Emotions,* [23] emotions such as joy and interest help us to flourish by broadening the array of thoughts and actions that come to mind whenever we feel them. Joy, for example helps us to go further by unleashing the desire to play, be creative, and push the limits of our experience. The emotion of interest helps to broaden our capabilities through encouraging us to explore, take in new information and experiences, and expand our sense of who we are and what we can become.

In pursuing our ruling passion we deepen our knowledge, joy and sense of wonder of the possibilities that lie ahead of us.

When we love what we do and are deeply interested in learning more about it, we find ourselves *moving with passion*. This emotive energy and moving force can carry us an extremely long way. This is something that Terry Byrne, the man whose journey we explored at the beginning of this chapter knows well. Byrne followed his ruling passion. He committed himself to being the best he could be, in every job he did, in an industry that he loved. Like Byrne, when we discover and continue to develop our own ruling passion, we grow in stature and the Ideal Way Forward grows and evolves with us, keeping us deeply absorbed in both what we love and what we know matters.

Applying the Third Master Move:

Through the Third Master Move we discovered that:

- Our true Ideal Way Forward awakens within us a deep sense of desire and feeling to follow its direction.

- The work we love to do becomes an autotelic experience – an end in itself. It creates intrinsic rather extrinsic motivation.

- When we are intrinsically motivated we free ourselves from distracting thoughts of reward and recognition and we become fully absorbed in what we do.

- The dopamine released in our brains when we do what we love, creates an inner feeling of joy and a powerful desire to repeat the experience and stay with our passion.

- By connecting our passion and our purpose, we create a twin source of motivation.

- By following our ruling passion – what we most love and what we are best at – competing desires and temptations lose their hold over us.

- The innate desire to know more and learn more about our ruling passion, keeps us engaged and aligned with our Ideal Way Forward, which continues to grow and evolve as we do.

To apply the Third Master Move you need to discover your ruling passion. If you are unsure of what it is - ask yourself, *what are my biggest strengths or talents?* And of these strengths or talents - ask yourself, *what do I most enjoy doing?* This will help you to narrow down to your ruling passion.

To then connect your ruling passion to your Ideal Way Forward (and your purpose), ask yourself, *how can I use my talent to make a bigger contribution to my life and work, and to the lives of the people that matter around me?*

It is important to remember, however, that following the Ideal Way Forward is not simply an intellectual pursuit. Doing what we love creates a *high feeling state* within us that joyfully (and not forcibly) binds us to this path. When we turn our faces toward the Ideal Way Forward, our genuine interest in this path keeps our attention focused there and our passion and love of what we do positively propels us along its course.

However, with the many stresses, pressures and temptations that beset the path of success, we need to make sure we can sustain the love for what we do so that we do not deviate from our Ideal Way Forward. To do this we need to *infuse* a sense of passion and enthusiasm into both our reflection and visualisation exercises.

When doing the evening review exercise we discussed in applying the First Move you will remember that it consisted of asking yourself the following three questions when reviewing the day's events before going to bed: *What worked? What didn't work? What do I need to change?*

To these three, now add the question: *What did I most love about my work or life today?* As you ask yourself the question make an effort to re-live the most enjoyable elements of how you performed in the day.

In his book *Buddha's Brain* the author and neuropsychologist Rick Hanson, suggests that paying more attention to the rewarding aspects of any experience helps to increase the dopamine levels in our brain. Holding these positive experiences for longer makes the relevant neurons fire and wire together more, ensuring that the experiences of what we most enjoy and are good at, leave a stronger and lasting impression on our brains. [24]

We can also infuse greater passion into our work by adding another powerful exercise into our daily routine: a *first thing visualisation of the day ahead* or what I simply call the *morning preview exercise*.

Waking up fifteen minutes earlier than you normally do (or setting aside this amount of time at some point at the beginning of the day) - look forward in your mind to the main events of the day ahead in the natural order in which they occur. See yourself performing at your best in these situations and enjoying what you do. Then see your actions ripple out into the future and imagine how they help to create the long term success you most desire in your life.

This morning preview exercise is a very effective way of setting up a progressive daily rhythm. It will help you to bring an enthusiastic intensity to whatever you do and will help to ensure your mind is *success rather than survival orientated.*

Once your ruling passion takes centre stage in your life it will create a sense of urgency within you to know more and learn more about it. I tell my clients that one of the acid tests that confirms that you have truly ignited your ruling passion is that you will have a feeling within you that even one whole lifetime is not sufficient for you to adequately pursue or bottom out your passion. The deeper you go, the more you will discover there is to learn.

This sense of urgency to know more about your ruling passion, however, needs to be finely balanced. You only have a finite amount of time and energy. There is a danger that if you pursue your passion too vigorously it can lead to burnout. To avoid this and to make the most of your time and physical energy:

- Take regular breaks throughout the day. Scientists say that our physical body is subject to 'Ultradian rhythms'; these are 90 to 120 minute cycles during which your body move from a high-energy state to a physiological low. At this point you need to take a break otherwise you will be begin to suffer from restlessness and tiredness and you will have difficulty maintaining adequate levels of concentration. [25] In my experience working regularly in a depleted energy state leaves us more susceptible to negative thoughts and the allure of unhelpful temptations, so it is vitally important that you discipline yourself to take time out to recharge and replenish your energy.

- This can be achieved through good nutrition, good exercise and good sleep. Your physical energy can also be greatly enhanced through ensuring your breathing is smoother and deeper. Oxygen is a major fuel of the body and especially the brain, which despite representing only 2 percent of your body weight, consumes 20 percent of your oxygen intake. [26] (Breathing consciously for a duration of time also helps your mind to enter a more poised and optimal state; see the Seventh Master Move – *Move with Poise*)

- Finally you can greatly enhance your productivity by ensuring that your attention is highly focused in these high intensity work cycles by avoiding distractions and being clear about exactly how you wish to use your time.

Ensuring that your physical energy meets the demands of following your ruling passion is essential and should not be overlooked. When you move with purpose and passion along the path directed by the Ideal Way Forward your progression will accelerate. Opportunities will come thick and fast but so too will many significant challenges. You will need to use your mental, emotional, and physical energy wisely as your capabilities and your desire to go further *will be tested.*

As we discover in the next Master Move you may reach a point in your journey when you feel you cannot go on. It may feel like the path of the Ideal Way Forward rises too quickly or too sharply for you to continue. It is then that you will need to *look inwards* rather than outwards for an inner strength that can carry you further. When you find it you will grow in presence, and you will know that you possess the key to unlock a greater wave of success.

---

[1] See the online article: http://www.dohafilminstitute.com/press/robert-de-niro-advises-young-actors-don-t-expect-to-be-famous-you-have-to-love-what-you-do-and-have-fun-doing-it

[2] See BBC online article by Andrew Benson, *Sebastian Vettel not satisfied with four F1 drivers' title,* 6 November 2013:
http://www.bbc.co.uk/sport/0/formula1/24838863

[3] Agassi, A., *Open: An Autobiography,* London, Harper, 2009, p3.

[4] Lyubomirsky, S., King, L.A., & Diener, E., *The Benefits of Frequent Positive Affect: Does Happiness Lead to Success?* Psychological Bulletin, 131, 2005, pp. 803-55.

[5] Csikszentmihalyi, M., *Creativity,* New York, Harper Perennial, 1996, p113.

[6] Lyubomirsky, S., King, L.A., & Diener, E., *The Benefits of Frequent Positive Affect: Does Happiness Lead to Success?* Psychological Bulletin, 131, 2005, pp. 823

[7] Marden, O.S., *Pushing To The Front,* originally published 1894. Reprint: Wilder Publications, 2007, p249.

[8] Syed, M., *Bounce,* London, Fourth Estate, 2010, p59.

[9] A good insight into the brain's reward system is given by the author Ian Robertson in his book *The Winner Effect,* London, Bloomsbury, 2012.

[10] Hanson, R., with Medius, R., *Buddha's Brain,* Oakland, New Harbinger Publications, 2009.

[11] The fact that neurons fire and wire together is something first observed by the psychologist Douglas Hebb: See Hebb, D.O., *The organization of behaviour,* New York, Wiley, 1949.

[12] Jeffries, S., *Why did Andre Agassi hate tennis?* The Guardian, 29 October 2009

[13] Agassi, A., *Open: An Autobiography,* London, Harper, 2009, p29.

[14] Robertson, I., *The Winner Effect,* London, Bloomsbury, 2012.

[15] Robertson, I., *The Winner Effect,* London, Bloomsbury, 2012, p24.

[16] Hagan, P., *Men lose their minds speaking to pretty women,* The Telegraph, 3 September 2009

[17] The Marshmallow or cookie experiment and its results are described in: Kahneman, D., *Thinking Fast and Slow,* London, Penguin, 2012, p.47

[18] Google search statistics are provided on: http://www.thinkwithgoogle.com/articles/search-insights-brand-power-tool.html

[19] *Satya Nadella named Microsoft CEO as Bill Gates steps down as chairman,* The Guardian Online: http://www.theguardian.com/technology/2014/feb/04/microsoft-satya-nadella-new-ceo

[20] Colvin, G., *Talent is Overrated,* Boston, Nicholas Brealey, 2008, p164-165

[21] Adrian Newey quoted in the Reuters online article: *Vettel can challenge Schumacher records,* 28 October 2013 : http://uk.reuters.com/article/2013/10/28/motor-racing-vettel-idUKL3N0II1D520131028

[22] Litsky, F., *Geena Davis zeros in with bow and arrows,* New York Times, 6 August 1999.

[23] Fredrickson, B.L., *The role of positive emotions in positive psychology: The broaden-and-build theory of positive emotions,* American Psychologist, Vol 56(3), Mar 2001, 218-226

[24] Hanson, R., with Medius, R., *Buddha's Brain,* Oakland, New Harbinger Publications, 2009. p69

[25] Schwartz, T., & McCarthy, C., *Manage your Energy, Not Your Time,* article originally published in 2007, presented in *HBR's 10 Must Reads, On Managing Yourself,* Boston, Harvard Business Review, 2010

[26] Hanson, R., with Medius, R., *Buddha's Brain,* Oakland, New Harbinger Publications, 2009. p185

Master Move 4
Move with Presence

The road to confidence

The birth of courage

A belief in something

Outer and inner strength

Greater presence

The need to grow

Why we play it safe

> *In the face of great challenge,*
> *Inspired Movers show great presence.*
> *Acting with belief, courage and*
> *confidence they galvanise themselves*
> *and their chances of success.*

The need for more presence

The discovery of our Ideal Way Forward in life gives us great impetus. Pursuing our ruling passion gives us, as we have seen, great joy. The positive state we reside in, when our passion and purpose unite, can make us feel as though anything is possible. Our success feels assured – at least for a while – and we entertain loftier dreams about the future.

It is then, when riding high and when enjoying a certain degree of success, that circumstances can suddenly change. Knocked by some unexpected blow we can find ourselves grounded again. As the American Poet Walt Whitman wrote, "It is provided in the essence of things, that from any fruition of success, no matter what, shall come something to make a greater struggle necessary." Life brings a new challenge to our door and what we do with that challenge will define us. When tested, will we expand or contract? Will we seek victory over circumstance, or will we be consigned to a depressing fate?

More often than not, the situation I describe in the opening paragraphs of this chapter, is what often precipitates my work with a client. Sometimes individuals will seek out a mentor, psychologist or performance coach like myself - when faced with a great opportunity that they wish to capitalise on; more often, however, a client requires my help when facing a *great challenge*. At such a time, they deeply desire or require some form of personal transformation. Facing uncertainty about their future, they have a powerful incentive to change and are more open to it.

Generally speaking, most of us resist change due to two types of mental bias that economists and psychologists have identified, and which shape our attitude towards change. The first of these is what is referred to as a *status quo* bias: in essence we have a tendency to keep things as they are. Change requires effort and can be difficult, so we prefer not to change if we can help it. [1] As we shall discover in the Fifth Master Move, over time our behaviours and habits become more and more entrenched making change even harder.

The second type of mental bias that shapes our attitude towards change is the *loss aversion* bias. Researchers have shown losing something generally makes us twice as sad as gaining the exact equivalent would make us happy. It is a feature of the mind that the Nobel Prize winning psychologist Daniel Kahneman illustrated using an experiment that he devised along with a colleague. [2] Broadly speaking, they put a simple question to those involved in the experiment: on the flip of coin, if heads you lose $100, and tails you gain a higher amount of money, how much would this higher amount need to be for you to accept the bet? Kahneman found that in most cases the typical answer was $200. In other words we need the prospect of winning $200 to overcome the aversion of losing $100.

This loss aversion bias means we have strong propensity to stick with what we have. Or in other words, *we play it safe*. So long as nothing material changes in our lives, the status quo and loss aversion biases hold sway over our thinking; until, that is, we face a great challenge that drastically alters our future landscape. We then realise that *without change* the success we desire may elude us.

We possess an inclination to keep things as they are. Great opportunity or uncertainty, however, opens the door to great change.

We have to become more than we currently are, if we hope to stay on course with the Ideal Way Forward. We cannot afford to shrink in these moments. To meet the challenge we need to grow and move with greater presence.

Defining greater presence

When we speak of individuals like business leaders, for example, having 'presence' we may be immediately drawn to their physical stature; they often seem tall in height. In his book *Blink* Malcolm Gladwell states that 58 percent of CEOs of Fortune 500 companies – the largest organisations in the United States – are six feet or taller. This compares with a figure of 14.5 percent for men in the wider U.S. population. The statistic gets more pronounced the taller you go: a third of CEOs, for instance, are six foot two or taller compared to an average of 3.9 percent for adult men in the wider U.S. population.[3] Gladwell suggests that Fortune 500 CEOs are taller than average not as a result of some deliberate prejudice but possibly as a result of an unconscious bias or implicit associations we have about height and leadership. Gladwell observes:

Most of us, in ways that we are not entirely aware of, automatically associate leadership ability with imposing physical stature. We have a sense of what a leader is supposed to look like, and that stereotype is so powerful that when someone fits it, we simply become blind to other considerations. [4]

However, our perceived physical stature isn't merely a function of height and neither is the presence we convey. The sense of how tall someone is can be subjective. In their bestselling book, *The Definitive Book of Body Language*, the authors Allan and Barbara Pease explained why some short movie stars or politicians are perceived as being taller: they simply *act taller* or give bigger or more powerful performances. [5] In other words they use their physical posture to project presence and to make themselves appear *larger than life*.

If we adopt a more confident body posture not only do people's perceptions of us change, but as Amy Cuddy - the Harvard Business School social psychologist - reports, it also has a discernible and positive effect on both our brain chemistry and behaviour. Cuddy's research into body language suggests that by adopting what she refers to as "power poses" (imagine Superman in his classic feet spread and hands on hip posture) for a duration of even two minutes, reconfigures the brain in a beneficial way and helps us to become more assertive and more likely to take the risks that are necessary in the pursuit of success. As Cuddy states:

...the best leaders — both male and female — seem to have relatively high testosterone, which is linked to decreased fear and increased tolerance for risk and desire to compete, and low cortisol, which is linked to decreased anxiety ... by "power posing," or adopting expansive, open non-verbal postures that are strongly associated with power and dominance across the animal kingdom, for just two minutes before entering a high-stress situation, people (both men and women) can increase their testosterone by about 20% and decrease their cortisol by about 25%. [6]

Interestingly, Cuddy's research suggests that "faking" a power pose in the way she describes - even when we are not confident - can still create a more favourable brain chemistry that can help us to perform better in job interviews or other stressful situations. Her findings certainly seem to have a struck a chord; her excellent talk on TED about her power pose research has been watched nearly fifteen million times. Manifesting enhanced presence is something that clearly interests many of us: our ability to compete and succeed in high pressure situations depends upon it.

However, whilst a powerful use of body language can certainly uplift our presence and 'standing tall' can give us a short term psychological boost, presence is about more than physical stature. In my experience it flows from a deeper source. I define presence as: *the outward projection of the genuine level of inner strength we feel.*

When we find our source of inner strength, it is something we can feel within us *and* something palpable that others can feel *radiating* from us. It is this, that I refer to as *great presence*. When we move with this presence, we move with a feeling of power and strength that adds great weight to our character.

Great presence may project outward for all to see.
It flows, however, from the deep reserves of
strength within us.

The late-Nelson Mandela - one of the great leaders of our time - is an excellent example of someone who powerfully embodied great presence. Following his death in December 2013, the American congresswoman Maxine Waters, described what it was like to be in the presence of the revered South African leader:

Mandela was a kind of person that you were so in awe of until you were almost stymied in your ability to speak with him on an ordinary level... Most of the time I was with Nelson Mandela, I was listening to him. He was the one with the experiences, he was the one with the history, he was the one who had sacrificed and he was the one who... was revered by everybody and sought after by everybody in the world. [7]

Waters hinted at what made Mandela's presence so notable: it was his rich experience and history. As a result of his 27 years of incarceration Mandela was someone who suffered exceptional hardship in his lifetime and yet despite this, over the period of his long ordeal, he developed the inner strength and equanimity to deal with the trying circumstances he faced. As Mandela himself revealed, his optimism and belief in a brighter future was his source of strength and success:

I am fundamentally an optimist. Whether that comes from nature or nurture, I cannot say. Part of being an optimist is keeping one's head pointed towards the sun, one's feet moving forward. There were many dark moments when my faith in humanity was sorely tested, but I would not and could not give myself up to despair. [8]

Mahatma Gandhi, another of the 20th century's great leaders, exuded great presence through his moral courage to fight an unjust occupation of his homeland, in a dignified and peaceful way. As Howard Gardner wrote in his book *Leading Minds:*

Gandhi's greatest contributions extended well beyond the Indian subcontinent. Through his inspiring writings and his own embodiment of personal courage, he conveyed to people around the world that it is possible to resist in a way that is honorable, does not involve counterattack, and may even bring resolutions that empower all concerned. [9]

Gandhi and Mandela were both exceptional leaders. The great presence they radiated outwards strengthened their resolve to face their respective difficulties and gave hope to a whole nation of men and women who were touched and empowered by their presence. The ordeal each of them faced ultimately shaped their character. Each found an *unshakeable* inner strength – the source of their great presence – at times when they were tested most by outer circumstances.

As so many of us discover, sooner or later, difficult circumstances that temporarily weaken us also provide the means to build greater strength; and the challenges which test us most are often the one's that unleash our deepest reserves of strength and energy. For example, one of the most difficult challenges we can face is losing a parent at an early age - an experience which can be deeply unsettling. However, as the award winning journalist Daniel Coyle has suggested, it can also prove to be a significant stimulus for an individual to succeed in life. In his excellent book *The Talent Code,* Coyle quoted research compiled in the 1970s (by the clinical psychologist Martin Eisenstadt) which showed that a significant number of notable high achievers over the course of history, had lost a parent at an early age:

Julius Caesar (father, 15), Napoleon (father, 15), fifteen British prime ministers, Lincoln (mother, 9), Gandhi (father, 15), Copernicus (father, 10), Newton (father, before birth), Darwin (mother, 8), Dante (mother, 6), Michelangelo (mother, 6), Bach (mother and father, 9), Handel (father, 11), Keats (father 8; mother, 14) Emerson (father, 8), Nietzsche (father, 4), Twain (father, 11) [10]

In addition to Eisenstadt's names, Coyle provided a comprehensive list of recent showbusiness stars who have lost a parent before the age of 18 including: Eddie Murphy, Steve Allen, Madonna, Paul McCartney, Bono, Cate Blanchett, Daniel Day Lewis, Sir Ian McKellen, Julia Roberts and Robert Redford. Coyle suggests that losing a parent triggered a *primal response* in these individuals; they suddenly felt unsafe in the world, leading to a significant release of motivational energy as they attempted to secure their means of survival. In Coyle's words: "tripping the ancient self-preserving evolutionary switch, provided energy for their efforts, so that they built their various talents over the course of years, step by step."

Whilst contending with death is one of life's defining challenges - every adversity that tests our capabilities, our desire, and our commitment, causes us to dig deep and find more within ourselves. Stoic philosophers of old knew this well. As Seneca said, "The good things which belong to prosperity are to be wished, but the good things that belong to adversity are to be admired." [11] Every adversity brings with it the chance to develop what I believe are the three main features of great presence – *Belief, Courage and Confidence*. As we shall now see, all three of these qualities are interlinked.

The power and limits of belief

When faced with difficulty Inspired Movers invariably rise to the challenge. Take Roger Federer for example – another well-known personality that radiates great presence. As Boris Becker, the six-time tennis Grand Slam singles champion, observed, Federer has an aura about him on court that Becker suggests comes from the confidence gained through winning multiple Grand Slam titles. [12] However, despite Federer's immense talent his success wasn't always a foregone conclusion.

Early in his career Federer had a habit of succumbing to pressure at key moments of big matches, and some tennis commentators began to doubt whether he'd ever reach the top of the game; instead they wondered if he would end up joining the ranks of the nearly-men who never quite fulfil their potential.

To compete at the highest level, Federer had to find greater belief to help steady himself in big pressure point situations. As Federer himself revealed, later in his career, "I always knew I had it in my hand – the question was: do I have it in my mind and my legs? That's something I had to work extremely hard at." [13] As Becker alluded to, Federer's presence on court comes from winning battle after battle, win after win, and title after title. However, before Federer won the first of his major titles he needed to *believe* that he could win. As his record 17 Grand Slam titles pay testimony to, it was a battle he won.

Like Federer, many other Inspired Movers have had to overcome the challenge of others doubting their ability; for example many doubted whether Jerry Rice, the greatest receiver in NFL history, was quick enough to play in the NFL. He was, as a result, passed over by fifteen teams in the 1985 draft before the San Francisco 49ers finally signed him; Wilma Rudolph, the American sprinter and winner of three gold medals at the 1960 Olympics suffered from polio as a child which impaired her ability to walk and caused many doctors who treated her to doubt whether she would ever recover; Thomas Edison, one of the greatest inventors of all time, was a sickly child whose intelligence was doubted by his teacher who considered Edison to be retarded; Walt Disney was famously fired by a newspaper editor because he believed Disney was "lacking imagination and had no good ideas"; Richard Branson's father doubted his son's early entrepreneurial exploits and wanted him to pursue a career in law like he had done; and before J.K. Rowling became one of the bestselling and highest earning authors of all time, her parents believed that her "overactive imagination was an amusing personal quirk that would never pay a mortgage, or secure a pension".

The challenge of belief represents a major hurdle for all of us at some point or other - especially in situations that require us to perform at a higher level than we have done before. At such times, belief can often feel like an intangible quality; sometimes we have it and feel empowered to rise to the challenge that confronts us, whilst at other times we can fall victim to doubt and literally feel the belief drain away from us, leaving us in a psychologically weaker and disempowered state. This feeling of being strengthened or weakened by belief is not just a subjective state of mind. Neuroscientists have proved that it has a *physical* basis: belief or the lack of it affects our brain chemistry which in turn affects how we feel and behave.

We have already seen, through the power pose research, how physically putting ourselves in a more confident physical posture enhances the testosterone flowing through our brains which makes us feel more assertive and dominant. When we genuinely believe we can succeed in a situation, the added security and happiness we feel also enhances our dopamine level (the brain's reward chemical we came across in the last Master Move) – which boosts our alertness, attentiveness and ability to deal with challenges. The brain also produces serotonin, which enhances our mood, and adrenaline which provides a greater surge of energy and helps to boost our performance levels. [14]

Belief therefore, and the positive cocktail of brain chemicals it produces, has an immediate effect on our mental, emotional and physical capabilities, as does its opposite - doubt. When we find ourselves in situations that we think are too challenging or beyond our capability, we feel more insecure and stressed. This causes the brain to release the hormone cortisol which limits not only our mental potential but can also have a debilitating effect on our physical wellbeing if we suffer too prolonged an exposure to it.

Coming back to the situation facing the young Roger Federer, and all the other Inspired Movers mentioned who were doubted at some stage, they all needed to demonstrate that they could perform at a higher level and mix it with the best in their profession. To do this they needed to believe that they were *better* than their doubters were giving them credit for.

Even the greatest amongst us are doubted until they succeed. Inspired Movers remain secure in their belief of what is possible.

This act of 'believing we are better' *before* we have proved to the world that we are, is one of *the* key obstacles in the path of success. Without having an inner belief in our abilities, the way we think others view us, or judge us, can massively hinder our progress in life - as demonstrated by two revealing research experiments.

The first involved a large number of both high and low-caste boys from rural villages in India, who were asked to solve a number of puzzles. [15] In the first round of the experiment all the boys completed the tests without having to disclose their caste to each other. The results showed that both the low and high-caste boys did more or less equally well. However, before the experiment was to be repeated for a second time, each boy was asked to confirm a public announcement which detailed his name, village, father's and grandfather's name and crucially in terms of the experiment, his caste. The boys were then given more puzzles to do but this time a significant gap in performance opened up between the two groups – the performance of the low-caste boys showed a marked decline.

The second experiment - a classic within the field of psychology - was carried out in 1968 by Jane Elliot, an American schoolteacher.[16] Quoting some made-up study, Elliot told the students in her class that research had shown that people with blue eyes were more intelligent and more likely to be successful than people with brown eyes, who were, according to this same made-up research, of inferior ability. She then divided the class into blue-eyed and brown-eyed groups, giving extra attention to the blue-eyed students. The outcome was fascinating. The blue-eyed group quickly began to dominate their 'inferior' brown-eyed classmates, showing also an improvement in their school performance. Simultaneously, the brown-eyed group began acting submissively and experienced a decline in performance. A few days later, Elliot told the class she had got her wires crossed and it was actually the brown-eyed people that were superior – leading to a complete reversal in the performance of the two groups.

Both the caste system and the blue eyes-brown eyes experiments reveal how our belief in ourselves can be heavily governed by where we believe we stand in life's pecking order. There is a real danger that we might ultimately limit our ability to compete with those we feel are 'better' than us, if we accept that we will *permanently* occupy a lower position in some arbitrary or man-made hierarchy.

In all spheres of life, a hierarchy of some description is found operating whether it is the social hierarchies of primates, the organisational chart of a large business, league tables or rankings in professional sport or the most pervasive of all, mankind's status hierarchy (that we explored in the Second Master Move) in which so many compete to gain a higher foothold.

Generally speaking, hierarchies of any description can be stress-infused environments where those higher up seek to assert their dominance by pushing down on those below them. For example, in the everyday parlance of business, sport, or some social network, people can refer to someone lower down the pecking order who has bright or ambitious ideas as 'having ideas above his or her station'. Or there is often talk of putting someone 'back in their place' should they have the temerity to compete with someone higher up the rankings. In these situations the individual who believes he or she has the most power, talent or ability is empowered and enjoys the hormonal advantage of greater levels of testosterone and dopamine; the individual who believes he or she is less, in any way, loses out and suffers from an increase in cortisol [17]– the stress hormone – and discovers that his or her ability to move with any degree of presence is literally diminished.

An interesting insight into how low status can affect brain chemistry was demonstrated by scientists who examined the dominant and subordinate behaviour of macaque monkeys [18] after they had taught the monkeys that they could self-administer cocaine by pressing on a lever which provided them with as much or as little of the substance as they desired. The outcome of the experiment was fascinating. Dominant and higher ranking monkeys had higher dopamine levels in their brain and took significantly lower amounts of cocaine than the lower ranking and subordinate monkeys, who had to offset their power or dopamine deficiency by consuming more of the cocaine.

Given how hierarchies can dominate our thinking and our behaviour, belief is an essential quality for those of us who want to rise up the ranks of our profession or, better still, break free from the insidious effects of an enforced hierarchy. *In every hierarchical encounter there is a battle waged within us between belief and doubt.* To win this battle, we have to believe we are better than our present circumstances or our standing, as life portrays it. We have to believe we have more potential within us. We need to galvanise ourselves with this greater belief so that we do not – like the cocaine-hooked macaque monkeys – seek some artificial means by which to boost our sense of worthiness or self-esteem.

But how can we build the kind of inner belief that gives us the courage to rise through the ranks, or defeat formidable opponents and overcome our biggest challenges?

The belief that leads to courage

In times of our greatest doubt, trials, or tribulations, we often look up to some form of higher power that we hope can confer upon us greater strength and capability; some form of superior intelligence and energy that can raise us beyond the limits, constraints, or the stranglehold of a man-made hierarchy that threatens to hold us back or keep us down.

We are uplifted when we hear the bible or some other revered text (or divine authority) tell us that, "for him that believes anything is possible". Or, if we have a more philosophical rather than spiritual or religious inclination, we take hope from some great mind such as Ralph Waldo Emerson, who told us that, "What lies behind us and what lies in front of us pales into comparison to what lies inside of us". It is beyond the scope of this book to explore all the various belief systems that can give us faith but, as I say to all the individuals I work with, it is important that we *believe in something;* something that is bigger in size and potential than we are today; a strength or power that we feel we can tap into; most importantly, something that has logic and meaning to us *individually*.

In my experience beliefs can be very personal and our reasons for believing in them can be very subjective; for example as one of my clients (an entrepreneur, who from nothing, generated personal wealth running into tens of millions of pounds) told me, "My brothers and I were raised in a poor family but my grandmother made us believe and feel as if we were kings. As a result I never once felt inferior to anyone. I succeeded because of this belief."

*To become more than we are today, we must
believe we possess a greater capability within us.*

Regardless of their subjective nature, empowering beliefs have a deeply positive effect on our thinking and it is for this reason that we need to believe in something. As we have seen in this chapter, belief gives us access to a more powerful brain chemistry that is instrumental in helping us to move with greater presence.

However, there is something we all possess that we can universally believe in and draw inspiration from: it is the amazing potential that resides in the human brain. Neuroscientists tell us it is composed of about 100 billion nerve cells or neurons - each of which can make somewhere between a thousand to ten thousand connections with other neurons. These points of contact (called synapses) are the communication points where information gets shared between neurons. All the possible permutations of brain states that these connections between neurons allow, is so remarkably large that it *exceeds* the number of elementary particles in the known universe. [19]

The sheer complexity of the brain affords it great potential but one of the really exciting developments in neuroscience, which has great relevance to us all, is that the brain is not hardwired as first thought. Brain scientists use the word *"neuroplasticity"* to describe the fact that the brain is highly *malleable* and has the remarkable ability to *rewire* or *reorganise* itself.

As the next Master Move will reveal, what we do and the way we think literally shapes the brain, and just like a muscle the more we work or train a certain area of it, the stronger and faster it gets. As Anders Ericsson – the world's foremost authority on expert performance, whose research we discussed in the First Master Move – and his colleagues point out, intensive practice can profoundly influence nearly all aspects of the human body such as the muscles, nerve and cardiovascular systems, and the brain. [20] The fact that the brain can rewire itself is leading to the discovery of 'scientific miracles' that would not be out of place in a science fiction book. As the psychiatrist Norman Doidge shared within the best-selling neuroscience book *The Brain that Changes Itself*:

I met a scientist who enabled people who had been blind since birth begin to see, another who enabled the deaf to hear...I met people whose learning disorders were cured and whose IQs were raised; I saw evidence that it is possible for eighty-year-olds to sharpen their memories to function the way they did when they were fifty-five. I saw people rewire their brains with their thoughts, to cure previously incurable obsessions and traumas. I spoke with Nobel laureates who were hotly debating how we must re-think our model of the brain now that it is ever changing. [21]

Doidge's words – backed by the rigors of science – provide encouragement to us all. The brain holds the veritable key to all success. Every move we make, from the mundane to the inspired is fashioned within it. As we saw when discussing the Second Master Move, it allows us to imagine a better vision of our future. Crucially, when it comes to our present concern of how to manifest more belief, it allows us to imagine a better version of ourselves. The two are deeply related. The Ideal Way Forward for each of us requires us to call forth and express our *Ideal Self*.

Whether we believe in divine potential, human potential or the brain's potential, this Ideal Self is the very best conception of ourselves that we can hold *steady* in our minds. This inner image isn't necessarily just the best of who we are today, it also incorporates an image of the best we *believe* we can become *in time*.

Our Ideal Self fulfils the Ideal Way Forward.
We must believe in the best we can become
to express it in what it is we do.

In my experience, very few of us consciously hold an image of our Ideal Self at the forefront of our mind. Instead we downplay, doubt, or (worse still) completely overlook our present or future capabilities. As a result I find that a great degree of my work with my clients is invested in helping them to find an alternative and better conception of themselves, that is grounded in both their current experience and a genuine belief of who, or what, they think they could become. It is when they believe that *more is possible* in their imagination and correspondingly, when their Ideal Self becomes a *definite* and *believable* image in their minds, that another quality springs forth within them and that is *courage*.

Courage and belief combined have remarkable effects on our body and mind. Our presence feels noticeably enhanced. Every challenge, test or competitive encounter that stretches our capabilities - which may have caused us angst in the past - is now seen as an opportunity to unleash an exciting aspect of our Ideal Self that we haven't as yet expressed. Moreover, when courage galvanises our hearts and minds, we find we are able to overcome two of life's biggest fears that otherwise threaten to thwart our progress: the *fear of failure* and the *fear of public opinion*.

The late Steve Jobs was an excellent example of someone who understood the fearlessness that belief and courage can instil in both an individual and an organisation. Jobs had an ability to create what some of his colleagues referred to as a "reality distortion field"; by that they meant he had a charismatic and persuasive ability to convince both himself and others that anything was possible. It was this belief that gave Jobs the significant courage which, as one journalist described, enabled him to set aside any fear of failure:

Of all that Steve Jobs' achievement has taught us, the importance of courage is especially relevant now. I don't mean his courage in facing his health issues, though that will be a story in itself if we ever learn the details. I mean his extraordinary courage as a business leader. Time and again, as the CEO of Apple, he introduced products, services, and entire business models completely unlike anything in existence. He disdained market testing (thus keeping his plans secret), he could not be sure he would succeed, and he risked significant losses and ridicule if he failed. [22]

Jobs had the courage to go it alone. He was prepared to *step up and stand out*. By doing so he was able to avoid the 'much of a muchness' that we so often see in people, performers or businesses; this homogeneity results from something that in the business world is referred to as *competitive convergence* - a situation whereby companies that do not have the innovative instinct (or courage) to try anything new for themselves, default to imitating the moves that others have made before them.

However, competitive convergence is not solely a feature of business; in the entertainment industry for example, Donna Soto-Morettini - a leading casting director – highlights the issue that many drama-school graduates come across as competent, pleasant and polished in auditions but do not have the necessary 'it' factor. The 'it' factor she suggests is the kind of strong performance that usually involves taking a little risk. [23] The greatest Inspired Movers, like Jobs, have to - at some time or another - take the risk that comes from breaking free from the pack and going it alone. They have to learn how to fashion their own moves. They have to follow an Ideal Way Forward that takes them off the beaten track. For a time their divergence from the pack can leave them open to criticism (or ridicule) from less able competitors or cynical opponents who themselves prefer the safety and comfort of the herd. Veering away from the path of convention, they have to contend with comments such as *"you're brave!"* or *"rather you than me!"* whilst also putting up with the negative expectation (and, as sad as it is to say, sometimes the perverse hope) of some, that they may crash and burn for entertaining what these cynics may suggest is some form of *Icarus Complex*.

Belief and courage together build formidable inner strength. Through them we overcome all that threatens to hold us back.

As Einstein once said, "Great spirits have always encountered violent opposition from mediocre minds" or as Ralph Waldo Emerson pointed out, "Pythagoras was misunderstood and Socrates, and Jesus, and Luther, and Copernicus and Galileo, and Newton... to be great is to be misunderstood."

When we go it alone, we have to contend with the uncertainty and the fear of failure that this courageous act of stepping up, or stepping out, brings with it. This can be a testing time for even the strongest amongst us and can lead to an inner voyage of discovery in which we get to know who we truly are. This voyage is often what the world of fiction and films refers to as 'The Hero's Journey'. It represents our biggest challenge and richest opportunity to build the kind of inner strength that in time shines outwardly as great presence.

The courage that leads to confidence

All the great movies we have seen, or stories we have read, involve the main protagonist of a story having to come face-to-face with a challenge that will make or break him (or her). The Hero's Journey is the path of growth or evolution for this central character. Christopher Vogler – a veteran story consultant for major Hollywood film companies – described it well in his book *The Writers Journey*:

At heart, despite its infinite variety, the hero's story is always a journey. A hero leaves her comfortable, ordinary surroundings to venture into a challenging, unfamiliar world.... But there are many stories that take the hero on an inward journey, one of the mind, the heart, the spirit. In any good story the hero grows and changes, making a journey from one way of being to the next: from despair to hope, weakness to strength, folly to wisdom, love to hate, and back again. It's these emotional journeys that hook an audience and make a story worth reading.
24

As Vogler touched upon, The Hero's Journey is one of great personal transformation and soul searching. More often than not this personal voyage involves some formidable struggle or battle that shapes the hero's character and, in time, secures his or her greatest triumph. One of the best known examples of The Hero's Journey in contemporary popular culture is the Harry Potter book series which charts the challenges and the eventual coming of age of the young wizard Harry. The stories have universally captured imaginations with worldwide sales of the books surpassing 400 million copies. [25]

The success story of the Harry Potter books is remarkable; however, it is perhaps eclipsed by The Hero's Journey of its author, J.K. Rowling. At the time Rowling began work on the first Harry Potter book, she had in her own words, experienced failure on an "epic scale"; she was a single parent, without a job, who was staring in the face of poverty. As she eloquently and honestly revealed in a 2008 talk she gave at the Annual Meeting of the Harvard Alumni Association:

... failure meant a stripping away of the inessential. I stopped pretending to myself that I was anything other than what I was, and began to direct all my energy into finishing the only work that mattered to me... Failure gave me an inner security that I had never attained by passing examinations. Failure taught me things about myself that I could have learned no other way. I discovered that I had a strong will, and more discipline than I had suspected... The knowledge that you have emerged wiser and stronger from setbacks means that you are, ever after, secure in your ability to survive... Such knowledge is a true gift, for all that it is painfully won, and it has been worth more than any qualification I ever earned. [26]

Rowling's early failures led her to undertake one of life's most valuable and character building exercises - *an honest appraisal of oneself.* This act of stripping your character bare, and ruthlessly examining the qualities it does or does not contain, is something that very few are willing to do. Given the tendency of the human ego to inflate its own capabilities, who we *think* we are, or *say* we are, is often different to who we *actually* are. This is often a pronounced feature of the kind of mind that forever believes it is capable, and frequently declares it's capability to the world ("If I wanted to, or had the time, I could do this or that or something great"); but such a character rarely puts itself in a position of risk, discomfort and danger that would ultimately reveal its true capabilities. The result is that until it is actually tested in some way, or by someone, it is happy to entertain and draw comfort from these sorts of self-deceptions or self-delusions.

It was the courage to view herself without any self-delusion, or indeed self-pity, that gave Rowling the clarity and impetus she needed to complete the work that mattered to her and which eventually brought with it such unrivalled success. In particular, her ability to *confront the worst-case scenario* and adopt a philosophical stance towards failure helped her to learn from her setbacks, rather than being consumed or crushed by them. In time her *courage* to keep going and follow through on her *belief* in herself, allowed her to develop her talent, which in turn gave her *confidence* in her ability. As the Harry Potter books flew off the shelves Rowling *knew* without doubt that she was a great writer. Every Inspired Mover, be it a Mahatma Gandhi or Nelson Mandela or J.K. Rowling or Roger Federer, has to go through this cycle of belief, courage and confidence in order to secure the success that matters to them. If we ourselves hope to create success and fearlessly walk the challenging path that the Ideal Way Forward directs, we need to continually immerse ourselves in this cycle.

It is through belief that we behold future possibilities. It is through courage and confidence that in time we achieve them.

With belief we can hold before ourselves the image of the Ideal Self that we hope to become. With courage we can attempt to bring forth the aspects of this Ideal Self that we haven't - as yet - fully expressed. With confidence we can fearlessly execute the moves and the proven capabilities we know we possess. Every time our belief leads to courage, and our courage leads to confidence, our inner strength is galvanised. It is then that we move with, and radiate, great presence.

Applying the Fourth Master Move:

Through the Fourth Master Move we discovered:

- Our loss aversion and status quo biases result in a tendency to keep things as they are.

- Great opportunity or great uncertainty provide the incentive we need to change and enhance our presence and sense of who we are.

- Presence is more than just our physical stature although embodying outward physical confidence can lead to a stronger inner state.

- Presence may be defined as the *outward projection* of the genuine level of *inner strength* we feel. It consists of three elements: belief, courage and confidence.

- Belief augments our inner strength and through positively affecting our brain chemistry it enhances our physical, emotional and mental capabilities.

- The Ideal Way Forward, for each of us, requires us to call forth and express our *Ideal Self* – the best we believe we can become.

- Our belief in our Ideal Self gives us the courage to express its qualities.

- Belief begets more courage and courage in time begets more confidence. It is by continually immersing ourselves in this cycle that we grow and move with presence.

As we discovered at the beginning of this chapter, your sense of presence can be boosted to a degree by adopting more expansive and confident bodily postures. By consciously making an effort to 'stand tall' and physically expressing yourself with more confidence you can change your brain chemistry in ways that are more favourable to risk-taking and making assertive moves.

Given the growing evidence that a more confident physical stature can enhance how we feel about ourselves, you may also wish to experiment with a mind-body exercise that appeals to you such as Qigong, Yoga, or martial arts that have power poses *embedded* within them. These types of exercises also have other additional benefits. Qigong for example has been shown, through scientific research, to reduce the effects of aging, minimise stress hormone levels in the body, and increase the strength of our immune systems. [27]

A more stable and secure feeling of presence (or inner strength), however, is something I believe we need to *earn*. It can be gained through meeting adversity and challenge head on, and learning and growing through these experiences. In other words we need to become more than we presently are.

To do this, you firstly need to believe you have - within you - more potential and greater capability. Ask yourself: *What is the underlying source of my potential? Is it a higher power or a belief in the power of the human brain or mind? How much do I believe in this power? What gives me faith in it?*

Once you are clear about why *you* believe in yourself, add the following visualisation into the morning preview exercise that we introduced into our daily schedule in applying the last Master Move:

- Sitting in a comfortable position on a chair, or the floor, and making sure your spine is upright, take a few moments to relax and ensure that your breathing is deeper and more rhythmic.

- Imagine you are somewhere where you feel inspired or somewhere that gives you a feeling of strength. Enjoy residing in this inner space for a few minutes and imagine yourself drawing in strength from your surroundings. Tell yourself that this space you have created within yourself is *free from all doubt and negativity*; it is the inner sanctum within which you are able to *imagine and experience what 'more' is possible.* Feel your presence and sense of self expand with this thought and then let go of the scene but make an attempt to retain the inner feeling of strength.

- As we did in the last Master Move, look forward to the main events of the day ahead and see yourself performing at your best and enjoying what you do.

- But now ask yourself: *If I really believe in myself what more is possible today?* Observe how this question changes your perspective on the day ahead. What qualities does this extra belief in yourself bring? Make a real attempt to see how these qualities express themselves through you. What are you thinking, feeling, saying or doing that is better than before?

- After you have enjoyed seeing this *belief-enhanced* preview of the day ahead, take it further by asking yourself: *If I really believe in myself **and** I am prepared to work hard to make any necessary changes what more could I achieve in the future?* As you did before, *see and feel* what more is possible.

- Seeing and feeling yourself expressing greater potential, affirm to yourself: *"With greater belief, I am more........."* Complete the sentence by stating (either verbally or internally) the qualities that you are expressing. For example, seeing yourself making clear, well-informed and powerful decisions in a situation that deeply matters to you, you could say: "With greater belief, I am more decisive, bold and clear in my actions" or seeing yourself overcoming some great challenge or competitor, you could say "With greater belief, I am more resilient and strong. I always persevere to the very end".

- This belief-enhancement exercise is an excellent way to experience your Ideal Self, which is an image of the best you believe you can become. The exercise will help you hold this image steady in your mind on a daily basis and *works on many levels.*

- Using the word *"if"* (e.g. *If I really believe,* or *If anything is possible* or *If nothing could hold me back…what could I attempt, create or accomplish? etc.)* allows you to more freely access your imagination. Seeing and feeling an imagined state that you desire has a tangible effect on you. It will bring with it greater enthusiasm and courage to express your Ideal Self. Regularly using the affirmation "With greater belief, *I am* more…" is a powerful declarative statement. By declaring *you are* something makes it *real in your imagination*; this is really important because to achieve anything significant, you have to first believe it in your imagination before you can manifest it in reality.

The Ideal Self that you hope to become also has a significant bearing on the evening review exercise we introduced in the First Master Move. When closing out each day with this exercise, now also ask yourself, *How bold was I today in expressing my Ideal Self? Could I have achieved more with greater courage?*

This exercise helps you to honestly appraise how your current self compares with your Ideal Self. It will allow you to be more objective about who you are today. Looking at yourself without any sense of self-delusion requires courage but it also provides tremendous clarity. You will become increasingly clear as to the scale of any challenge before you and what needs to be done to close the *gap* between where you are now and where you hope to be in the future.

Closing this gap is where our attention now turns. Belief holds up the image of our Ideal Self. Courage gives us the stimulus to express this Ideal Self to the degree we can become it today. However, to manifest confidence we need to close the gap between what we *think* is possible and what we *know* is possible.

In my experience, we can frequently confuse the terms belief and confidence and use them as if they mean the same thing. *But belief is not confidence.* Belief grows from what you *think* is possible in your life – the aspects of your Ideal Self that you haven't as yet fully expressed. Confidence on the other hand flows from what you *know* is possible – from the moves that you know you possess and have performed time and time again.

Developing a serene inner confidence is what carries us further along the Ideal Way Forward. If we are not to leave our success to chance, we need to be confident in our ability to unleash the optimal moves when it most matters most to us. As we will see in the next Master Move the highest levels of performance – that bring the greatest rewards and deepest satisfaction – require us to master our craft and *move with precision.*

---

[1] Samuelson, W., & Zeckhauser, R., *Status Quo Bias in Decision Making,* Journal of Risk and Uncertainty, 1988, I :7-59,

[2] Kahneman, D., & Tversky, A., *Choices, Values and Frames,* New York, Cambridge University Press, 2000.

[3] Gladwell, M., *Blink,* London, Penguin, 2006, p87.

[4] Gladwell, M., *Blink,* London, Penguin, 2006, p88.

[5] Pease, A., & Pease, B., *The Definitive Book of Body Language,* London, Orion Books, 2004, p325.

[6] Cuddy, A., Want to Lean In? Try a Power Pose, HBR Blog Network: http://blogs.hbr.org/2013/03/want-to-lean-in-try-a-power-po-2/

[7] USA Today Online article: Members of Congress recall power of Mandela's presence, 5 December 2013: http://www.usatoday.com/story/news/politics/2013/12/05/congress-mandela-waters-conyers/2456299/

[8] Mandela, N.R., *Long Walk To Freedom: The Autobiography of Nelson Mandela,* London, Abacus, 1994

[9] Gardner, H., with Laskin, E., *Leading Minds,* New York, Basic Books, 2011, p259.

[10] Coyle, D., *The Talent Code,* London, Arrow Books, 2009, p113.

[11] The Seneca quote was mentioned by Sir Francis Drake in his essay "Of Adversity"

[12] Boris Becker interview for the Tennis Space website: http://www.thetennisspace.com/becker-exclusive-how-to-have-presence-on-court/

[13] Bower, C., *Roger Federer, the greatest,* London, John Blake Publishing, 2011, p136

[14] The effect of the brain hormones or neurotransmitters is described in several good books including: Wilkinson, R., & Pickett, K., *The Spirit Level,* London, Penguin 2010/ Doidge, N., *The Brain that Changes Itself,* London, Penguin, 2007 / Robertson, I., *The Winner Effect,* London, Bloomsbury, 2012 / Hanson, R., with Medius, R., *Buddha's Brain,* Oakland, New Harbinger Publications, 2009

[15] Hoff, K., & Pandey, P., *Belief Systems and Durable Inequalities: An experimental investigation of Indian caste,* Policy Research Working Paper, Washington DC, World Bank, 2004.

[16] Peters, W., *A Class Divided: Then and now.* New Haven, Yale University Press, 1987.

[17] Robertson, I., *The Winner Effect,* London, Bloomsbury, 2012, p147.

[18] Morgan, D., Grant, K.A., Gage, H.D., Mach, R.H., Kaplan, J.R., Prioleau, O., Nader, S.H., Buchheimer, N., Ehrenkaufer, R.L., Nader, M.A., *Social dominance in monkeys: dopamine D2 receptors and cocaine self-administration.* Nature Neuroscience, 2002, 5 (2): 169-74

[19] Ramachandran, V.S., *The Tell-Tale Brain,* London, Windmill Books, 2011, p14.

[20] Feltovich, P.J., Prietula, M.J., & Ericsson, K.A., *Studies of Expertise from Psychological Perspectives,* in *The Cambridge Handbook of Expertise and Expert Performance,* eds. Ericson, K.A, Charness, N., Feltovich, P.J., and Hoffman, R.R., Cambridge, Cambridge University Press, 2006, p59.

[21] Doidge, N., *The Brain that Changes Itself,* London, Penguin, 2007.

[22] Colvin, G., Needed: More of Steve Jobs' courage, CNN Money Website, 30 August 2011: http://management.fortune.cnn.com/2011/08/30/we-need-more-of-steve-jobs-business-courage/

[23] Morettini, D.S., *Mastering the Audition: How to perform under pressure,* London, Bloomsbury, 2012, p41.

[24] Vogler, C., *The Writers Journey,* Studio City, Michael Wiese Productions, 2007, p7.

[25] Flood, A., *Potter tops 400 million sales,* The Book Seller, 17 June 2008.

[26] A transcript of JK's Rowling talk, entitled The Fringe Benefits of Failure, and the Importance of Imagination can be found at:

http://harvardmagazine.com/2008/06/the-fringe-benefits-failure-the-importance-imagination
[27] Yan Lei, S., *Instant Health: The Shaolin Qigong Workout for Longevity,* China, Yan Lei Press, 2009

Master Move 5
Move with Precision

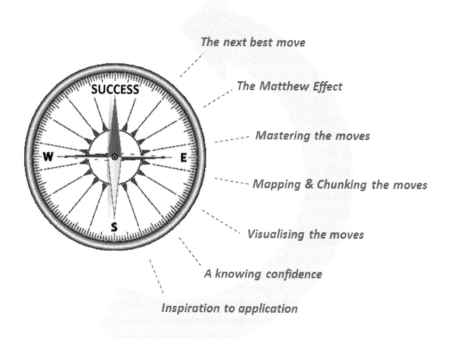

The next best move

The Matthew Effect

Mastering the moves

Mapping & Chunking the moves

Visualising the moves

A knowing confidence

Inspiration to application

*Inspired Movers visualise and master
the optimal moves that will bring
success; through hard work and
refinement they execute these moves
precisely and effortlessly.*

Inspiration, aspiration and application

The journey so far in this book has been one of *inspiration* and *aspiration*. Inspiration comes from knowing our Ideal Way Forward – the personal form of success we desire most. Aspiration comes from knowing our Ideal Self – the best we believe we can become.

We have now, however, reached a definitive point in our bid to unleash Inspired Movement. To reach higher levels of success, we must turn inspiration and aspiration to *application*. Application comes from mastering the moves that we imagine our Ideal Self to possess and which we believe can create the success we desire.

You will remember, from part 1 of the book, that I defined the high performance state of Inspired Movement as:

The ability to make the optimal moves at the right time and the right place, in any situation, by moving in complete alignment with the Ideal Way Forward

In the first four Master Moves we have explored how we can create alignment to the Ideal Way Forward through:

- *Moving with progression*: knowing that success is achieved gradually over time.

- *Moving with purpose*: knowing what it is that we want to achieve, and why it is important to us.

- *Moving with passion*: connecting our purpose and our ruling passion – doing what we most love, and what we are best at, to accomplish what matters most to us.

- *Moving with presence*: staying true to our purpose and committed to our passion when we are challenged hard and we need to courageously express the greater potential of our Ideal Self.

As we now head into the final three Master Moves, we must turn our attention to the first component of the Inspired Movement definition. We must learn how to perform the actual moves that will *achieve* the Ideal Way Forward. Specifically, success in any situation depends on:

- Knowing the precise combination of moves that will achieve the outcomes we desire.

- Having confidence that we can execute these moves as efficiently and as effectively as possible.

The self-assurance of the one who knows

When we are unsure of what to do - at any moment - life instantly appears more complicated. Our thinking becomes clouded. The immediate future seems obscure. Belief and courage may empower us to take bold steps forward, but the fact remains that we cannot confidently stride on to success until any mental fog clears. We need clarity in these moments; we need to know the moves that can help us see off a challenge or capitalise on an all important opportunity. In short, we need to know what to do and how to do it.

As an old proverb says, "Authority flows from the one who knows". The word authority can have many meanings but one definition of it is: *the confidence derived from experience or practise.* Experiential knowledge gives us a feeling of authority and self-assurance in situations where we can put this knowledge to good use. When we know we have the right moves and are confident that we have got what it takes, we can then take command of a situation and exercise greater influence over what happens next. Like Michael Jordan we can make the shots that take control of a game or like J.K Rowling we can write the story that shapes our future.

With belief we think we can succeed.
With confidence we know we can.

The fictional character of Sherlock Holmes – like real life Inspired Movers - exudes confidence. Sherlock 'flows' from his sharp and vast intellect. The film director Guy Ritchie, however, took Holmes' self-assurance to another level in his big screen adaptation of the character in the 2009 film *Sherlock Holmes*. Ritchie's Sherlock Holmes (played by Robert Downing Jr) is not only a supreme thinker but also a streetwise fighter who possesses absolute conviction in his moves.

In one brilliantly conceived scene, Holmes is in the middle of a bare-knuckle boxing match with a giant of a man (named McMurdo) when he sees Irene Adler – his love interest – in the crowd. Desiring a quick exit, Holmes tries to forfeit the fight and is about to walk out of the boxing ring when McMurdo spits at the back of his head. Holmes tells himself not to let McMurdo's vulgarity register on an emotional level, and then imagines - in slow motion and vivid detail - *precisely* what he intends to do next. The exact combination of moves he visualises to take out McMurdo are (in summary):

Move 1 – Distraction:

Distract opponent by throwing a handkerchief in his face.

Move 2 – Discombobulation:

Daze opponent by striking his left cheek, clapping hands over his ears, and following up with a shot to the body.

Move 3 – Devastation:

Two more blows to the opponent's body, a right hook to his jaw, finishing with a heal kick to his chest. [1]

As Holmes concludes his visualisation he mentally runs through a detailed diagnosis of McMurdo's future condition: "In summary: ears ringing, jaw fractured, three ribs cracked, four broken, diaphragm haemorrhaging. Physical recovery: six weeks. Full psychological recovery: six months. Capacity to spit at back of head: neutralised."

Having seen the end from the beginning, Holmes then executes all his imagined moves with exact precision and sends McMurdo flying out of the ring with his final kick to his opponent's chest. The direction of the scene is graphic but it does reveal something important: *for the man who knows what to do there is clarity, for the man in the dark there is confusion* – or as Holmes might say, discombobulation!

Seeing the moves of success

Guy Ritchie's Sherlock Holmes is just a fictional character but the manner in which he visualises the moves he intends to make, reflects the inner workings of a high performing mindset. Neurological studies have shown that imagining something in vivid detail fires the actual series of neurons or brain cells that would normally come into play when you physically do what you are imagining. [2]

Repeatedly visualising yourself performing a desired combination of moves not only strengthens these neural networks (by helping them to fire and wire together) but as researchers at the University of Pittsburgh and Carnegie Mellon University have shown, mental visualisation also beneficially activates the pre-frontal cortex in the brain – the executive centre we discussed in the Second Master Move. As they discovered, greater visualisation of an action results in better performance when it comes to executing the action. [3]

What we see more vividly in our imagination,
we can create more precisely in reality.

The tangible and positive effect visualisation has on the mind and brain, is something Inspired Movers within professional sport use to great advantage. As we discussed earlier in the book, the American diver Laura Wilkinson won a gold medal at the 2000 Olympics (despite being injured in the run up to the games) by sitting on the diving platform for hours at a time and running through detailed visualisations of her dives in her mind. Other Inspired Movers have also used such visualisation techniques to imagine the combination of moves that ultimately brought them great success. For example, the legendary NFL coach Bill Walsh – who led the San Francisco 49ers to three Super Bowl victories – revealed in his book *The Score Takes Care of Itself,* how precise visualisation helped him prepare for games. As Walsh described:

At San Francisco our first twenty or twenty-five plays of the game would be scripted, along with a multitude of options, alternatives, and contingency plays depending on the situation and circumstance. Among other things, it plugged me into the future; I was visualizing the game ahead, "seeing" what would happen. I could close my eyes and literally see all twenty-two men running and responding to some specific play I had drawn up. [4]

Jonny Wilkinson, one of the best goal-kickers in Rugby Union history, revealed his success in the game also came from an exact inner vision of how to work his signature move:

The psychology of kicking is so important. You must visualise where the ball is going to go. Then you have to be able to trace that line from between the posts to the exact spot of the ball, and see that in your mind's eye when you go to kick the ball. Then I visualise the ball travelling along that path and imagine the sensation of how the ball is going to feel when it hits my foot for the perfect strike. [5]

The exceptionally talented Brazilian footballer, Ronaldinho – a player famed for his dancing feet and an ability to conjure up magical combinations of moves – revealed the detailed visualisation and planning work that he undertook before games that gave him the edge on a soccer field:

When I train, one of the things I concentrate on is creating a mental picture of how best to deliver the ball to a teammate... So what I do, always, every night and every day, is try and think up things, imagine plays, which no one else will have thought of, and to do so always bearing in mind the particular strength of each team-mate to whom I am passing the ball. When I construct those plays in my mind I take into account whether one team-mate likes to receive the ball at his feet, or ahead of him; if he is good with his head, and how he prefers to head the ball; if he is stronger on his right or his left foot. That is my job. That is what I do. I imagine the game. [6]

The use of detailed visualisation, however, is not a specific feature of the sporting mind. It is also used effectively by many creative performers and business leaders to build, in their mind, a clear story of the success they *intend* to achieve.

A remarkable example of this involves the actor Jim Carrey. In the late 1980s, when he was a broke and struggling actor, he decided to employ the use of visualisation in a bid to change his fortunes. As Carrey revealed on the Oprah Winfrey show [7] he would drive up into the Hollywood Hills and spend time alone imagining his future by focusing on details such as making a good impression on film directors and seeing them being interested in his work. Carrey also took the additional step of writing himself a cheque for $10 million dollars – "for acting services rendered" – and dated it Thanksgiving 1995. As Carrey told Oprah, his future materialised with an unerring accuracy: Carrey received $10 million dollars around Thanksgiving 1995 for his role in the box office hit *Dumb and Dumber*.

Oprah Winfrey herself – like her interviewee Jim Carrey – knows the power that is invested in a compelling vision. She has become a self-made billionaire media mogul in the United States and one of its richest and most influential women. Much of her success has been built on the highly popular Oprah Winfrey Show, which ran from 1986 to 2011 and which was syndicated to 212 U.S. television stations and in more than 100 countries worldwide. [8] The success of the show stemmed from Oprah's vision of what a compelling talk show should look like. In the early 1990s when all other similar shows were focused on tabloid gossip, Oprah saw the opportunity to build a show based on deeper themes such as social issues, literature, self-help, and spirituality.

Oprah's vision and affable nature quickly turned her show into America's number one daytime talk show and allowed her to build a $2.9 billion personal fortune; and secure her place in history alongside an exclusive group of self-made billionaire women such as the late Rosalía Mera ($6.1 billion) the Spanish entrepreneur who co-founded the high street fashion chain Zara, Wu Yajun ($4.3 billion) – the Chinese property developer, and Meg Whitman ($1.9 billion) – now the CEO of HP, but formerly the CEO of eBay.[9]

Oprah's success enabled her to imagine greater possibilities such as owning her own television network and using her wealth to create opportunities for more disadvantaged members of society – something which earned her the Presidential Medal of Freedom in November 2013 (the United States highest civilian honour awarded to her by President Barack Obama for her sizeable contribution to the country).

Oprah, like so many leaders in business, experienced abundant success from the use of visualisation or 'visioning' – as it is more often referred to within the corporate world. Entrepreneurs and CEOs use their visioning skills to build compelling images of the future through which they shape the future success of their organisations. Great visionary leaders such as Steve Jobs, Jeff Bezos – the founder of Amazon – or Larry Page and Sergey Brin – the co-founders of Google – have all built multi-billion dollar organisations by imagining compelling products or services that never previously existed.

Inspired Movers see their desired future ahead of time. They excel by seeing the moves before they make the moves.

Whether it is the world of business, sport, or entertainment the ability to visualise a desired outcome or future creates clarity. *Seeing the moves before we make the moves* increases our chances of success. Like Ronaldinho or Bill Walsh we can then "see the game, before we play the game" or like Jim Carrey or Oprah Winfrey we can visualise a more compelling future that brings with it great wealth and possibilities. However, we can't be vague in our imaginings. We can't leave important details to chance. We need to work up the precise moves that will give us the confidence to know we can succeed.

Working up the optimal moves

As we discovered in the Second Master Move – *Move with Purpose* – our chances of success are increased when we visualise both outcome and process goals in any situation where we desire success. The outcome goal is our Ideal Way Forward – it is the vision of what we hope to achieve. Process goals are the precise moves we imagine ourselves making that will achieve the Ideal Way Forward.

The visualisation accounts of Bill Walsh, Jonny Wilkinson and Ronaldinho that we read earlier were heavily focused on imagining the precise moves that would bring success; Walsh could see all twenty-two men running on a football field responding to some *specific* play he had drawn up; Wilkinson could trace the line from between the posts to the *exact* spot of the ball that he needed to make contact with; Ronaldinho could imagine plays that took into account the *particular* strengths or weaknesses of the other players around him. The ability of these Inspired Movers to focus on the 'specific', 'exact' or 'particular' details of an imagined situation allowed them to subsequently move with precision and perform at a higher level. In fact, researchers have shown that one of the defining differences between expert and non-expert performance across many disciplines is that experts set themselves more specific technique or process goals than non-experts. For example, in one research project that investigated the performance of volleyball players, high performers focused on technique goals such as 'toss the ball properly' whereas lower performers had general goals such as 'concentrate' or they worked with no imagined goals at all. [10]

In other words, high achievers know the *precise* moves that can create higher levels of performance and success. It is for this reason that I

121

ensure that whenever I work with my clients (regardless of whether they operate in professional sport, the corporate world or a creative field like the entertainment industry) that they have a clear process or *blueprint* in mind of the success they intend to achieve. Like Guy Ritchie's Sherlock Holmes it is important they can see the moves of success but also be confident that they can execute them with efficiency and precision. To help them achieve this I share with them a simple process to 'work up' their moves; it comprises of the following three steps:

- Step 1: Map the moves

- Step 2: Chunk the moves

- Step 3: Master the moves

Step 1 involves identifying the four to five headline moves that create a map (or an overarching process) of the success they intend to achieve. (For example, we broke Holmes' successful plan of attack against McMurdo into three clear moves: Move 1 – Distraction, Move 2 – Discombobulation, Move 3 – Devastation).

Step 2 involves breaking down each of these headline moves into their basic constituent parts or 'chunks'. [11] (For example, Holmes' second move, Discombobulation, involved three chunks: Chunk 1 – Daze opponent by striking his left cheek, Chunk 2 – Clap hands over his ears, Chunk 3 – Follow up with a shot to the body).

Step 3 involves the important work of repeatedly practising these moves so that they can be well executed when needed (something which we will come on to shortly).

Figure 5.1 provides an illustration of how the vital process of *mapping* and *chunking* the moves of success fits into our model of Inspired Movement:

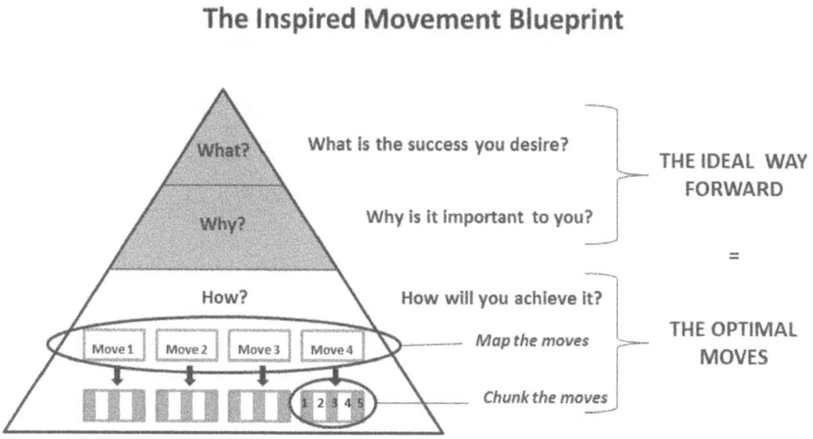

The Inspired Movement Blueprint

Figure 5.1

The Inspired Movement blueprint provides us with a useful framework within which we can outline the optimal moves that can create the success - and achieve the Ideal Way Forward - we desire in any situation. It allows us to visualise, at a higher level, any detailed plans that we may draw up to support our ambitions (that feed into and sit behind this blueprint).

The Ideal Way Forward, in effect, provides us with a clearly defined strategy and the process of mapping success into four or five headline moves (and then breaking each of these moves down into smaller manageable chunks) give us the *tactics* by which we can achieve our aims.

By using the blueprint in this way we can more clearly see the *what*, the *why* and the *how* of the success we are trying to achieve; regardless of whether we are using it to map a career path or the optimal moves that will allow us to outperform or outmanoeuvre a close competitor. When we are prepared in this way – and are *aligned* to our Ideal Way Forward – we can see more precisely what we need to do and we can be more confident that we have what it takes to succeed, when it is time to step up and perform.

---

*By mapping the moves of success we
gain clarity. By mastering them
we gain confidence and certainty.*

However, visualising our precise moves of success is not enough, like Guy Ritchie's Sherlock Holmes we need to be confident we can successful execute these moves when required. To do this we need to take action. As Jim Carrey told Oprah Winfrey he didn't just visualise and then "go make a sandwich" – he worked hard to make his vision a reality; or as Jonny Wilkinson revealed when speaking further about his visualisation work:

Whether we're two points down, or we need this kick to pull eight points ahead, I put the tee down, look at the posts and eventually, mentally, return to the training ground where I've done this thousands and thousands of times. That's what gives me confidence - the knowledge that I've done this before. [12]

True self-assurance only comes when we follow Step 3 of the process outlined earlier; we need to master our desired moves. Our confidence in them can only grow in proportion to how much we practise and refine them. Wilkinson was confident in his kicking because he had practiced it thousands of times. Given then the importance of Step 3, what is the best way to master our moves?

Mastering our moves

To be successful we must begin by mastering the basics of any move and evolve from there. This seems like an obvious statement but it is worth exploring a little as, in my experience, its importance is easily overlooked. As the acclaimed acting director Konstantin Stanislavski pointed out:

An actor, like an infant, must learn everything from the beginning, to look, to walk, to talk, and so on. ... We all know how to do these things in ordinary life. But unfortunately, the vast majority of us do them badly. [13]

Sometimes the basic moves that we make can seem so straightforward that we forget to pay attention to how well we perform them; the result is that we pick up bad habits that, more often than not, compromise our future potential in some way. Even elite athletes, for instance, can fall foul of not mastering the basics and can end up 'compensating' their technique and veering away from the most efficient biomechanical or ideal pattern of movement. As Joanne Elphinston – a leading physiotherapist and performance consultant – points out:

The problem with compensating is that while it initially appears to allow the athlete to perform a certain skill, it rarely yields optimal efficient performance over time. This is seen even in high performance athletes. Many athletic performance plateaus are associated with compensatory movement strategies that cannot support further development. The athlete may have demonstrated great potential or even achieved success at an early age, but a loss of form or a persistent barrier to improvement is eventually reached if the compensatory strategies are not addressed. [14]

As Elphinston suggests, quick progress (or the need for rapid success) may eventually curtail our future potential; or as Lao Tzu, the sixth century BC Chinese philosopher poetically expressed, "He who stands on tiptoe doesn't stand firm. He who rushes ahead doesn't go far."

The issue of seeking results too quickly is commonplace in fields such as politics, sport, business and entertainment where rapid success is the order of the day. This rush to get ahead can often lead to people finding expedient short-cuts to the top that cost them dearly in the end. Such individuals may give off the superficial impression that they have great depth but they are often left exposed when their range of moves is overwhelmed by the demands of challenging situation or a role for which they are not ready. This choice of expediency over excellence is often made by overly ambitious individuals who are heavily motivated by extrinsic rewards such as power, material wealth, or superficial recognition. To master our moves the first requirement is to go *slow* and understand the exact mechanics of what we're looking to do. Like Sherlock Holmes earlier, we need to run through our proposed moves in slow motion so that we can take in all their precise details. This is exactly the technique used by many top performers to perfect their mental and physical understanding of their desired moves.

In tennis, for example, the highly successful Spartak Tennis Club in Moscow (which has produced a string of top tennis talent including Mikhail Youzhny, Marat Safin and Anna Kournikova) uses a technique called *imitatsiya* to help its young players master their basic tennis strokes; it involves rallying in slow motion with an imaginary ball before players commence hitting the ball for real. [15] The use of slow and precise movements allows these players to *physically chunk* the major components of their backhand, forehand and serving strokes, and thereby ensure they are constructed with the right technique before they attempt to speed up their execution.

It is by first slowing down our moves that we can, in time, speed up their execution.

This ability to slow down and understand the exact mechanics of any desired move is a technique also used successfully in other fields. In music, for instance, the highly acclaimed Spanish concert pianist, Alicia de Larrocha, built up her mastery on the piano by playing difficult passages very softly and slowly, before later speeding up her technique once she became proficient at playing a particular piece. [16]

In the volatile and fast-moving world of business, Warren Buffett has enjoyed considerable success in stock market investment, by similarly taking his time. Not only is Buffett well-known for patiently delving into the fine detail of every business he invests in, but once he chooses a stock he holds onto it for a long period of time. Buffett is famous for saying, "If you don't feel comfortable holding a stock for ten years, you shouldn't own it for ten minutes." Going slow has allowed Buffet to understand the complexities of his trade.

In the field of writing, one of the most influential and best-selling success books of all time, *Think and Grow Rich* - which has sold over

70 million copies [17] since it was written in 1937 – is also a product of going slow. The book came into existence after Andrew Carnegie – one of America's richest men at the time, and one of its greatest philanthropists – asked a young journalist called Napoleon Hill, if he'd be prepared to spend *twenty* years of his life researching the 'secret of success' in order to take the message to the men and women of the world, who Carnegie felt might experience poverty or repeated failure without knowing this secret. Hill agreed, and spent the next twenty years interviewing over five hundred of America's most powerful and influential men and women including the likes of Henry Ford, Theodore Roosevelt, Woodrow Wilson, Thomas Edison, King Gillette, Alexander Graham Bell, John D. Rockefeller and F.W. Woolworth. Once Hill had fully grasped the complexities of creating success he wrote *Think and Grow Rich*, the essence of which he distilled into one of his most popularly ascribed quotes – "What the mind of a man can conceive and believe, it can achieve." [18]

Whether it is the process of conceiving, believing, and achieving, or the Inspired Movement journey of inspiration, aspiration and application, once we have conceptually grasped the chunks or the precise mechanics of our moves we need to practise them repeatedly so that we can execute them flawlessly and efficiently.

For example, once Buffet has made a decision to invest he needs to dynamically execute his trade, or when Ronaldinho or Bill Walsh have worked up a certain play in their mind they need to dynamically perform it at speed if they wish to outwit their opponents. We know from earlier in the book that success takes time and effort, so what expectations should we hold as to how long it will take or how hard it will be to master our desired moves?

As we discovered previously, the eminent psychologist Anders Ericsson suggested it takes a minimum of 10 years of intensive practice to achieve mastery in any complex field. It appears therefore that we cannot leave success to chance, or hope that we can rely solely on natural talent when it comes to mastering our moves. However, 10 years isn't necessarily a magic number as the author David Epstein brought to light in his fascinating book *The Sports Gene.* [19] For example, at the 2007 World Athletic Championships, Stefan Holm the Swedish High Jumper and 2004 Olympic gold medallist, was beaten by a young Bahamian high jumper called

Donald Thomas. As Epstein pointed out, Holm had logged over 20,000 hours of practise since taking up the sport as a young child. Thomas on the other hand had only taken up the sport less than a year earlier and had managed to clear a respectable height of 7 feet on his very first jump; it turns out Thomas has unusually large Achilles tendons that provide extra spring in his jump. As Epstein made clear, elite performance could take 3,000 hours, 10,000 hours or 20,000 hours and not just the 10,000 hours proposed by Malcolm Gladwell in his book *Outliers,* or the 10 years as suggested by Ericsson's research (to be fair to Ericsson, he himself concedes that when it comes to the 10-year rule, 10 is not necessarily a magical number and the amount of intense training required to become an internationally acclaimed performer differs across various professions).[20]

Epstein's aim isn't necessarily to dismantle Ericsson's research, but to show that the advantage of natural or innate talent cannot be dismissed outright. The nature versus nurture debate is a difficult one to 'bottom out' as success is likely to result from a confluence of many intricate factors such as genetics, upbringing, the influence of parents, mentors and teachers, the availability of opportunities, exposure to formative challenges, as well as a whole range of other subtle psychological and sociological factors. However, regardless of their academic, or nature versus nurture, standpoints nearly all researchers looking into the causes of exceptional performance agree on one thing: *you can't dismiss the power of hard work.* As the 19th century US President, James Garfield, said, "If the power to do hard work is not talent, it is the best possible substitute for it."

The power and hidden reward of hard work

Regardless of how much natural talent Inspired Movers did or did not initially possess, hard work always shines through as a consistent feature of most success stories. The actor Will Smith emphatically made this point when he was once interviewed on an American talk show and said, "I will not be out-worked! Period. You might have more talent than me, you might be smarter than me, you might be sexier than me, but if we get on the treadmill together there's two things (that are going to happen): you're getting off first or I'm going to die on that treadmill. It's really that simple." [21]

Smith's capacity to put in the work has given him the edge in a highly competitive entertainment industry. It's what has enabled him to rise from playing the light-hearted Will in the popular American television series *The Fresh Prince of Bel-Air* into a serious Hollywood actor (and not to mention rapper) who is currently ranked by Forbes as the most bankable star worldwide. [22]

Smith's prodigious levels of hard work mirrors the efforts and constant refinement that someone like David Beckham was prepared to put into his free kick taking, that Michael Jordan was prepared to put into shot-making, or Andre Agassi was prepared to put into his tennis strokes. The dedication (and endless hours of practice) that these Inspired Movers have put into mastering their moves is widely known but few people in my experience are willing (as we discussed in the First Master Move) to match that level of commitment and effort.

However, for those that *are* willing, there is a 'hidden' reward – of immense value – to be gained from working hard: the moves we attempt today, that require great effort, can in time be made *effortless*. This phenomenon has great significance – it is the mechanism by which we can literally *free* our potential.

The ability to make our desired moves effortless is derived from the two systems of thinking we all possess, that psychologists and neurologists refer to as *System 1* and *System 2*: [23]

- System 1 is fast, effortless, automatic, and requires little conscious control.

- System 2 is slow, and deliberate, and allows us to consciously think through complex situations.

System 1 generally operates through feelings and instincts and works in familiar situations that allow us to work on autopilot such as reading simple sentences, taking a leisurely stroll, or crucially (as we will come to) when performing any complex move that we have mastered.

System 2 swings into action when we need to figure out how to accomplish a difficult goal. However, as capable as System 2 is, it has a few major drawbacks: not only is it slow, but it requires effort to use and has noticeable capacity constraints as its operation is heavily governed by how well we can concentrate. (For example, as you read this sentence try to simultaneously count the number of letters in each word or try to remember your phone number in reverse).

System 1, on the other hand, is exceptionally quick – its main agent, the unconscious mind can apparently process 11 million bits of information per second. [24] The two systems, however, work hand-in-hand and are designed to minimise effort and optimise performance. [25]

Generally speaking we mostly use the effortless System 1, but call upon the services of System 2 when we need to *slow down* and think through a situation. It is for this reason that practicing our moves slowly and deliberately has such a beneficial effect; it activates the executive centre in the brain and gives us the opportunity to clearly impress upon it the *exact* move we are looking to master. By repeating our moves over and over again, we are able to sink them into our subconscious and effectively hand over their execution from System 2 to System 1 meaning that they can then be performed rapidly and automatically without much thought.

When our moves become automatic in this way, something *remarkable* happens in the human brain: neurological studies show that the brain activity associated with performing the moves actually *decreases*, as does the energy and attention required to perform them. [26] They have *literally* been made effortless in comparison to the effort that was needed to master them and as a result our mental and physical capacity is *freed* to do more work.

That which takes great effort to master will, in time, lead to effortless mastery.

The Greek philosopher Plato summarised the relationship between the level of effort and the output of that effort by saying, "Maximum work with least effort equals grace." On an aesthetic level this seems true of natural performers who effortlessly express their talent: imagine Roger Federer or the American sprinter Allyson Felix in full flight - two athletes renowned for their graceful movement. There is, however, another possible interpretation of Plato's words: *the ability to do more with less effort is a grace or gift.* The effective use of this gift may account for the phenomenon that is known across some academic disciplines as the *Matthew Effect* [27]– a term which refers to the phenomenon of the 'rich getting richer' or the 'accumulation of advantages'. It is derived from the biblical verse *Matthew XXV:29,* "For unto every one that hath shall be given, and he shall have abundance: but from him that hath not shall be taken away even that which he hath".

The Matthew Effect has been used to describe situations where individuals who enjoy an advantageous start go on to accrue greater and greater benefits over time. For example, in the field of education it is used to describe the cumulative advantage that is gained by children who read well from a young age and learn more words and accrue more knowledge versus children who read more slowly and with less enjoyment (and whose reading abilities are, as a result, curtailed). [28] As one research paper commented, "the least motivated children in the middle grades might read 100,000 words a year while the average child at this level might read 1,000,000. The figure for the voracious middle school reader might be 10,000,000 or even as high as 50,000,000." [29]

Malcolm Gladwell used the Matthew Effect to describe the advantage gained by young children who initially perform better than their peers and who subsequently get the best teaching, the most attention, and greater access to training and coaching facilities. This, over time, gives them access to bigger and better opportunities than the children who showed less early promise. [30] However, not wanting in any way to trivialise the disadvantage faced by young children who do not show early promise or worst still are denied or have little opportunity to develop their potential, I personally think of the Matthew Effect (and the biblical verse that inspired its use) in a slightly different context. I think it is possible for *all* of us, relatively

131

speaking, to experience our own Matthew Effect. My interpretation of it is that: *for those that have (or hath) done the work, more is possible.*

The continued ability to work hard (and work intelligently) accrues greater advantages for those who are willing to put work in versus those that do not. For example, consider the career of the writer Isaac Asimov – one of the greatest and most prolific science fiction writers of all time. It took Asimov 19 years to publish his first 100 books, 10 years to publish the next 100, and then only 5 further years to take his total to 300 books. [31]

The ability to do more work, *by consistently putting in more work*, is seen in many disciplines, where beginners (or less committed performers), for example, can only manage an hour of intensive practice a day due to the heavy demands it places upon them. However, those that work hard to reach elite levels of performance, are able to undertake up to 4-to-5 hours of such practice daily. [32]

Or to use a more basic example, we experience the Matthew Effect when we train a physical muscle and find that it grows stronger and more efficient the more we work it. The Matthew Effect means that the greater the amount of work we put into mastering and expanding our range of moves the greater the possibilities. The ever-increasing rewards of the Matthew Effect may be one of the key reasons why Inspired Movers are prepared to put in the work. Desirable moves that are just out of reach today, or which take conscious effort to perform, can (with time and practice) be made simple and effortless. When our desired moves become effortless, we free our capacity to master bigger, better and more complex moves that open up greater possibilities that we can strive for.

Those that strive for more

The Matthew Effect means that, for all of us, *more is possible* - regardless of the level of innate talent or initial privileges we were (or were not) born with. This is a compelling thought and one that I personally feel is a better notion than the promise in some self-help books that *anything is possible*. It could well be that we could achieve anything (regardless of our current circumstances) but this concept can be too broad or too vast to apply easily. When we know that more is possible, we can begin to *map, chunk,* and *master* the next move that can enhance our level of performance or success. This form of *deliberate practise* [33] allows us to master the moves that are just outside of our current skill level but which can be perfected through intensive practise.

The desire to master the *next best move* is what sets Inspired Movers apart from lesser performers who often limit themselves by sticking to (and practising) what they know. For example, researchers have shown that elite figure skaters spend more time on challenging jumps than their lower-performing counterparts and make more attempts at jumps that they haven't yet mastered but need to perfect.[34] The result is they repeatedly fall on the ice. It is estimated, for instance, that Shizuka Arakawa – the Japanese 2006 Winter Olympic gold medallist – had to suffer at least twenty thousand falls onto the cold, hard ice on her long journey to Olympic success. [35] Arakawa may have drawn inspiration from an old Japanese proverb which states "Seven times down, eight times up" but to fall (and fail) twenty thousand times requires real spirit and resilience.

By sticking to what we know we limit our level. By striving for the next best move we raise the level.

It may have become one of life's platitudes but the ability to learn and grow from failure is a proven route to greater success. Mastering the most complex moves of our profession requires us to constantly refine our approach and strive for higher performance levels than we have previously demonstrated; the Formula One World Champion Sebastian Vettel is a great example of this. As Christian Horner – the Team Principal of Red Bull's Formula One Racing Team – revealed:

Sebastian is able to adjust, to understand what the car needs to go quick. He's not afraid to look at himself. To say: 'Where can I be better? What can I improve? What can I do to be a better driver?' Even if we have won a race, he's looking at his own performance and he is hugely self-analytical and that's a key element and extremely refreshing to work with, because he's totally honest in his approach. [36]

Sebastian Vettel, Shizuka Arakawa, and all other Inspired Movers, are constantly striving for the next best move; they do not stand still. It may be that they intuitively understand the meaning of the second part of the Matthew Effect – "but from him that hath not shall be taken away even that which he hath". Using the alternative interpretation of the Matthew Effect that we have adopted, we could say that: *for those that have not done the work, their current and future potential is lost.* Or, as it has been more colloquially put, 'Use it or lose it!'. Anders Ericsson observed this phenomenon in his research on expertise. As he pointed out:

It is well known that athletes and musicians who reduce or stop their regular practice will exhibit a reduced level of performance – a maintained level of challenge and strain appear necessary to preserve the attained physiological and cognitive adaptations. [37]

Inspired Movement rests upon our ability to keep on putting in the work. Even for the best of us there appears to be little option of coasting. The hugely talented Michael Jordan, for example, discovered that he had lost his edge when he returned to basketball after a temporary stint playing baseball; his loss of form contributed to his team – the Chicago Bulls – being eliminated in the play-offs that year. Jordan responded honestly to the situation by saying, "You can't leave and think you can come back and dominate this game. I will be physically and mentally prepared from now on." [38] Jordan subsequently picked up his level and the Bulls won three NBA titles on the bounce. This need to keep on working our moves was perhaps best expressed by Arthur Rubinstein – one of the greatest ever concert pianists – who famously said, "When I don't practice for a day, I know. When I don't practise for two days, the orchestra knows it. And when I don't practice for three days, the world knows it." [39]

The Matthew Effect – and both its promise and warning – holds great significance for us all. We may not have been able to determine the exact nature of our present circumstances but the fact remains that, for all of us, *more is possible.* It is incumbent upon each one of us to master as many moves as we can and discover *precisely* what more we can achieve in our own lives. It is only by mastering our desired moves that we can bring to life the potential and promise of our Ideal Self. It is only then that we can confidently know that we possess the optimal moves that can achieve the Ideal Way Forward, and that we possess the means through which we can shape our success more precisely.

Applying the Fifth Master Move:

The Fifth Master Move revealed:

- Our success is dependent upon our ability to turn *inspiration* and *aspiration* into *application*.

- Inspiration comes from knowing the Ideal Way Forward - the success we want to achieve in any situation.

- Aspiration comes from knowing our Ideal Self - the best we believe we can become.

- Application comes from mastering the moves that we imagine the Ideal Self to possess and which we believe will create the success we desire.

- Success ultimately comes when we can perform the optimal moves that achieve the Ideal Way Forward.

- To move with precision we need to: *map the moves, chunk the moves* and *master the moves of success*.

- Mastering the moves requires great effort but the 'Matthew Effect' combined with the ability we possess to make our moves more effortless means that more is possible for each of us.

- Inspired Movers and the best amongst us are constantly seeking to master the next best move that brings with it greater performance and enhanced success.

To begin the process of mastering your optimal moves of success, draw up as *detailed* a plan as you can of *how* you intend to create the success you desire, in a particular situation. Research (or where possible speak to) others who have achieved similar success. Ask yourself, what clear measures did they take to create their success? What specific moves helped them achieve their desired outcomes? If any of these moves involved detailed or complex techniques, research as thoroughly as possible what these techniques are by consulting the relevant books, online resources, and if possible the best technical teachers or coaches you can access.

If you are serious about creating a high level of success do not rush this stage of detailed planning and definitely consider *investing* in a technical coach. (Within my performance coaching practice I ensure my clients regularly consult the right technical coaches who can advise on the specialist aspects of the success - or high performance state - we are looking to create, so as to ensure any specialist moves are built on the right techniques).

The purpose of creating this detailed plan is to *expand* your understanding of how you intend to achieve your desired success. However, to help you consolidate this plan in your mind and to make it more usable, the next step is to *contract* this knowledge into the *Inspired Movement blueprint* I shared with you earlier (see Figure 5.1).

Draw out the blueprint (as large as you can) on a piece of A4 or A3 paper and write out the answers next to the questions: *What is the success you desire? Why is it important to you?*

Then, from the detailed plans you have drawn up, attempt to *map* in four to five headline moves (if possible) of *how you will achieve the success you desire.* Mark these moves on the Inspired Movement blueprint as per Figure 5.1. Try to make the wording for these headline moves as brief but as *memorable* as possible.

The next step is to *chunk* each move into its basic components, so that you can easily remember the important and precise details of how you intend to achieve your desired aims.

To help you visually, create your Inspired Movement blueprint see Figure 5.2 (at the end of this chapter) in which I have drawn up an imaginary blueprint for Sherlock Holmes' plan of attack against McMurdo that I described earlier.

Once you have created this 'success blueprint' put it somewhere where you alone can see it and review it often. Remembering, the *what* and *how* of your intended success will ensure you're aligned to your Ideal Way Forward (and the precise moves that can get you there). Remembering *why* your success is important to you will keep you *locked in* to your source of motivation.

In addition, visualise yourself as *vividly* as you can, performing the moves of success that you have mapped and chunked. Use this detailed visualisation to augment the *belief-enhanced morning preview exercise* we discussed in the last chapter, so that you can see and feel *precisely* what more is possible in the day ahead or in the immediate future.

Where possible, especially when you're looking to consolidate or master a new move it will be beneficial to visualise your Inspired Movement blueprint a number of additional times in the day. By imagining the new move in accurate detail, you will leave a greater impression on your brain (through greater arousal in your prefrontal cortex) which in turn will increase the likelihood that you will attempt the new move when the opportunity presents itself for real - rather than defaulting to what you have always done.[40]

In addition to your visualisation work it is *vitally* important that you *physically practice* any new desired moves so that you can master and perfect their execution. It is important to note, however, that changing your tried and tested moves in favour of better ones is a difficult task and should not be underestimated. Your System 1 and System 2 modes of thinking have made *everything* you have repeatedly done (both good and bad) effortless over time. Generally speaking, when faced with a choice, your brain follows the line of least resistance and will do what it has always done because it represents the line of least resistance and effort.

As the psychologist Daniel Kahneman points out, a general "law of least effort" applies to mental as well as physical exertion. [41] The law asserts that if there are several ways of achieving the same goal, people will eventually gravitate to the least demanding course of action.

To overcome the tendency of repeating habitual but undesirable moves you have to follow a *line of greater resistance* and make a conscious effort to impress upon your brain (especially the fast and effortless System 1) that there is a new move - *of greater value* – that you want to master. To do this:

-   Set aside additional time in your schedule to physically practice any new desired moves (over and above the time you set aside to maintain your existing moves). Begin by running through the new move in slow motion and by mentally talking yourself through its main chunks. When you feel ready you can then speed up your practice to the desired level and practice the move as a whole.

- Set clear process goals for your practice sessions (as discussed in the Second Master Move). Try to obtain accurate feedback every time you practise your new moves and keep a record of how well you are progressing. (For highly advanced moves that require intricate technique, a technical coach is an imperative if you're serious about achieving your Ideal Way Forward).

Most important of all, be clear in your mind that the ability to move with precision – by mapping, chunking, and mastering your moves- requires tremendous effort. To earn the right to compete alongside the very best in your field you must put in the level of work that the likes of Will Smith, Oprah Winfrey, Warren Buffet, Sebastian Vettel or Michael Jordan have put into developing their passion. Success cannot be left to chance. As we shall see in the next chapter, it is only when you have mastered your moves and made them effortless, that you can free yourself to look ahead and see the right place and the right time to work your moves to their greatest effect.

Holmes' Inspired Movement Blueprint

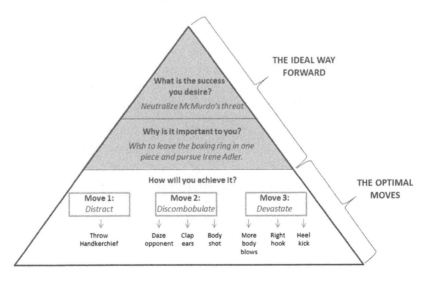

Figure 5.2

[1] The film does not portray the scene as Move 1, Move 2, etc. The demarcation into three broad moves has been used simply for illustrative purposes. An exact script of the scene is available online at http;//www.imdb.com/title/tt0988045/quotes

[2] Kreiman, G., Koch, C., & Fried, I., *Imagery Neurons in the Human Brain,* Nature 408 (2000), pp357-361

[3] The University of Pittsburgh and Carnegie Mellon University research is quoted in Goleman, D., Boyatzis, R., & McKee, A., *Primal Leadership,* 2001 featured in *HBR 10 Must Reads: On Managing Yourself,* Boston, Harvard Business Press, 2010.

[4] Walsh, B., *The Score Takes Care of Itself,* New York, Portfolio, 2009, p 50.

[5] The Guardian Online, *How to be the best kicker in the world,* 5 October 2003: http://www.theguardian.com/sport/2003/oct/05/rugbyworldcup2003.rugbyunion 13

[6] Ronaldhino quote taken from the article *Imagery in Sport,* featured on the sporting mind website: http://www.thesportinmind.com/articles/imagery-in-sport-elite-athlete-examples-and-the-pettlep-model/

[7] Jim Carrey's interview with Oprah on 17 February 1997 can be seen at http://www.oprah.com/oprahs-lifeclass/What-Oprah-Learned-from-Jim-Carrey-Video

[8] http://www.biography.com/people/oprah-winfrey-9534419?page=1

[9] http://www.forbes.com/sites/luisakroll/2013/03/06/the-rarer-sex-the-self-made-women-billionaires-of-2013/

[10] Zimmerman, B.J., *Development and Adaptation of Expertise: The Role of Self-Regulatory Processes and Beliefs* in *The Cambridge Handbook of Expertise and Expert Performance,* eds. Ericson, K.A., Charness, N., Feltovich, P.J., and Hoffman, R.R., Cambridge, Cambridge University Press, 2006, p708.

[11] This technique is actually called *Chunking.* It is a process of breaking down skilled performance; first outlined by the psychologists Chase and Simon with regard to expert performance in chess. See: Chase, W.G., & Simon H.A., *Perception in chess,* Cognitive Psychology, 4, 55-81, 1973a

[12] The Guardian Online, *How to be the best kicker in the world,* 5 October 2003: http://www.theguardian.com/sport/2003/oct/05/rugbyworldcup2003.rugbyunion 13

[13] Stanislavski, C., *An Actor Prepares,* London, Methuen Drama, p101.

[14] Elphinston, J., *Stability, Sport, and Performance Movement,* Chichester, England, Lotus Publishing, p24.

[15] Coyle, D., *The Talent Code,* London, Arrow Books, p82.

[16] Mach, E., *Great contemporary pianists speak for themselves,* Vols 1-2, Toronto, Dover, 1991

[17] Think and Grow Rich book sales quoted in the Forbes article: http://www.forbes.com/forbes/2011/0411/opinions-rich-karlgaard-innovation-rules-american-religion.html

[18] Hill, N., *Think and Grow Rich,* London, Vermillion, 2004 (original published in 1937).

[19] Epstein, D., *The Sports Gene,* New York, Penguin, 2013

[20] Ericsson, K.A., *The Influence of Experience and Deliberate Practise on the Development of Superior Expert Performance,* in *The Cambridge Handbook of Expertise and Expert Performance,* eds. Ericson, K.A, Charness, N., Feltovich, P.J., and Hoffman, R.R., Cambridge, Cambridge University Press, 2006, p689.

[21] See Will Smith interviewed on the Tavis Smiley show: see http://m.youtube.com/watch?v=AKWauRZ_LuI

[22] http://star-currency.forbes.com/celebrity-list/worldwide?page=0

[23] For an excellent insight into System 1 and System 2 thinking read: Kahneman, D., *Thinking Fast and Slow,* London, Penguin Books, 2011

[24] Coyle, D., *The Talent Code,* London, Arrow Books, p112. The fact that our unconscious minds can process 11 million pieces of information per second is quoted in research compiled by the psychologist John Bargh at Yale University (and his colleagues) who Coyle interviewed for the book. Bargh is a pioneer in the research of automaticity.

[25] The actual interaction between the two systems is complex and there is a possibility that the dual system model is overly simplified as it may not be possible to coherently link together all the attributes associated with System 1 and 2 respectively – see: Jonathan St. B. T. Evans, *Dual-processing Accounts of Reasoning, Judgement and Social Cognition,* The Annual Review of Psychology, 2008, 59: 255-78

[26] Kahneman, D., *Thinking Fast and Slow,* London, Penguin Books, 2011, p35

[27] The term was first used by the sociologist Robert Merton.

[28] Stanovich, K.E., *Matthew Effects in reading. Some consequences of individualsdifferences in the acquisition of literacy,* Reading Research Quarterly, 21, 360 -406

[29] Nagy, W.E., & Anderson, R.C., *How many words are there is printed school English,* Reading Research Quarterly, 19, 304-330, 1984.

[30] Gladwell, M., *Outliers,* London, Penguin, p30.

[31] Kellogg, R.T., *Professional Writing Expertise,* in *The Cambridge Handbook of Expertise and Expert Performance,* eds. Ericson, K.A, Charness, N., Feltovich, P.J., and Hoffman, R.R., Cambridge, Cambridge University Press, 2006.

[32] Colvin, G., *Talent is Overrated,* Boston, Nicholas Brealey, 2008, p201

[33] Deliberate practice is a termed coined by Anders Ericsson. See: Ericsson, K.A., *The Influence of Experience and Deliberate Practise on the Development of Superior Expert Performance,* in *The Cambridge Handbook of Expertise and Expert Performance,* eds. Ericson, K.A., Charness, N., Feltovich, P.J., and Hoffman, R.R., Cambridge, Cambridge University Press, 2006, p693

[34] Deakin, J.M., & Cobley, S., *A search for deliberate practice: an examination of the practice environments in figure skating and volleyball,* eds. Starkes, J., & Ericsson, K.A., (Eds.), *Expert performance in sport: Recent advances in*

research on sport expertise, Champaign, IL, Human Kinetics, 2003, pp 115-135.

[35] Colvin, G., *Talent is Overrated,* Boston, Nicholas Brealey, 2008, p187

[36] Richards, G., *Don't criticise Sebastian Vettel and Red Bull for doing their jobs,* The Guardian Online, 13 October 2013 :
http://www.theguardian.com/sport/blog/2013/oct/13/sebastian-vettel-red-bull-f1

[37] Ericsson, K.A., *The Influence of Experience and Deliberate Practise on the Development of Superior Expert Performance,* in *The Cambridge Handbook of Expertise and Expert Performance,* eds. Ericson, K.A., Charness, N., Feltovich, P.J., and Hoffman, R.R., Cambridge, Cambridge University Press, 2006.

[38] Michael Jordan quote taken from: Dweck, C., *Mindset – How you can fulfil your potential,* New York, Random House, 2006, p99.

[39] Arthur Rubinstein quote featured in: Gardner, H., *5 Minds for the Future,* Boston, Harvard Business Press, 2008, p43

[40] Goleman, D., Boyatzis, R., & McKee, A., *Primal Leadership,* 2001 featured in *HBR 10 Must Reads: On Managing Yourself,* Boston, Harvard Business Press, 2010.

[41] Kahneman, D., *Thinking Fast and Slow,* London, Penguin Books, 2011, p35

Master Move 6
Move with Perception

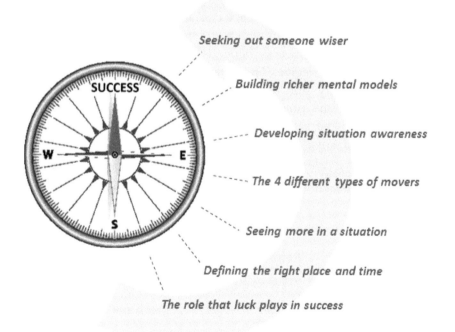

Seeking out someone wiser

Building richer mental models

Developing situation awareness

The 4 different types of movers

Seeing more in a situation

Defining the right place and time

The role that luck plays in success

Inspired Movers perceive more in a situation; they stay alive to the possibility that any moment may be the right place and right time to work their moves.

Luck, Providence and Success

So far we have learnt much that can accelerate our progress. But there is a fundamental skill which sits behind every Master Move - and upon which all success depends - that we have not (as yet) explored to a great degree. The greatest amongst us have developed this skill to a very fine degree. Inspired Movement is impossible without it. It is the power of *perception*: the ability - in any given moment - to make sense of what is happening around us and to discern what advantageous moves are open to us.

In his poem *I keep Six Honest Serving Men*, Rudyard Kipling, gave us the means by which we can enhance our power of perception, when he wrote:

I keep six honest serving-men

(They taught me all I knew)

Their names are What and Why and When

And How and Where and Who. [1]

In our Inspired Movement journey we have already inadvertently employed the services of three of Kipling's six honest men (otherwise known as the five Ws and one H). To achieve the Ideal Way Forward, we have discovered that you must know:

- *What* is the success you desire?

- *Why* is it important to you?

- *How* will you achieve it?

In this chapter, we will now put to good use two more of Kipling's men, by adding the following questions to our Inspired Movement blueprint: *Where* is the right place and *When* is the right time to make to make your moves? (see Figure 6.1)

The Complete Inspired Movement Blueprint

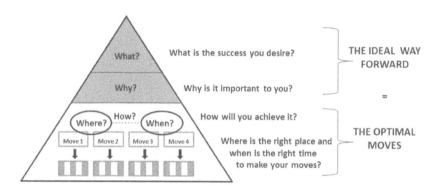

Figure 6.1

The last of Kipling's six honest men (*Who*) will make a defining appearance in the final Master Move but for now let's turn our attention back to the definition for Inspired Movement and specifically to the importance of seeing the 'right place and right time' to act, if we wish to create the success we desire.

The ability to be in the right place at the right time - and take maximum advantage of an opportunity when it presents itself - can often, in my experience, be put down to luck or serendipity rather than a keen sense of perception. For example, one of my clients who now runs his own successful consultancy business, was once overlooked for a senior role in a large organisation where he used to work, because the director interviewing him for the position felt there was a *"right place right time thing"* going on (with my client). In other words, the director was implying that his past successes were by luck rather than design.

The role that luck plays in the journey of success certainly cannot be dismissed; as the former England Cricketer, and now journalist, Ed Smith spoke of in his book *Luck: What it Means and Why it Matters,*[2] luck has played a role in the subtexts of many stories of success and failure (including his own). Smith explained how he was fortunate to be selected for England when injuries to key players gave him his chance but then how a poor umpiring decision called time on his England career and then later how a freak accident that broke his ankle ended his involvement in cricket altogether. Smith also touched on the role that luck has played in key moments in history. For example, Winston Churchill narrowly avoided death in 1931 when he was almost run over by a car; Smith argued that had Churchill's life been cut short at that moment, history would have judged him as a failed politician rather than the inspiring leader that he is now widely regarded as.

In his book, Smith also made reference to Margaret Thatcher – another celebrated British Prime Minister – and the fact that she was only able to run for the leadership of the Conservative Party after the leading candidate, Keith Joseph, scuppered his chances by making a highly controversial comment in one of his speeches which caused public outrage (Joseph had suggested that poor people should stop having so many children if they couldn't adequately support them).

In *Outliers*, Malcolm Gladwell also outlined the role that luck plays in success by describing how many successful individuals are invariably the fortunate recipients of "hidden advantages and extraordinary opportunities and cultural legacies that allow them to learn and work hard and make sense of the world in ways others cannot."[3] For example, Bill Gates – the founder of Microsoft – and Bill Joy – the co-founder of Sun Microsystems – were both fortunate to get early and ample access to the very first line of sophisticated computers (back in the late 1960s/early 70s) and were, as a result, able to learn advanced computer programming from a very early age. This advantage, Gladwell argued, was instrumental in them building their multi-billion dollar software companies. Drawing on other such examples of fortuitous circumstances Gladwell concluded that success is heavily dependent on being born in the right place and the right time, and into beneficial and advantageous circumstances. (As an aside, Gladwell has subsequently balanced his own take on success in his more recent book *David and Goliath* in which he recounts many 'against the odds' success stories where certain individuals have been able to capitalise on *"the advantages of their disadvantages"*)[4].

The psychologist Richard Wiseman, also explored the relationship between luck and success through a 10 year study during which he conducted a series of interviews and experiments with people who considered themselves to be lucky. [5] As a result of his findings Wiseman took a slightly different take on luck; in short, he concluded, luck is something that could be cultivated by having the right state of mind and by employing certain 'luck principles' such as believing you are lucky, expecting good fortune, and being able to transform bad luck into good luck.

Gary Player, widely regarded as one of golf's greatest players, also suggested that luck could be favourably induced, when he famously said, "The more I practise, the luckier I get," a quote which has become one of sport's most memorable and oft-repeated phrases. The Scottish mountaineer and writer, W.H. Murray took the concept of luck by design, rather than luck by chance, even further when he wrote:

Concerning all acts of initiative (and creation), there is one elementary truth, the ignorance of which kills countless ideas and splendid plans: that the moment one definitely commits oneself, then Providence moves too. All sorts of things occur to help one that would never otherwise have occurred. A whole stream of events issues from the decision, raising in one's favour all manner of unforeseen incidents and meetings and material assistance, which no man could have dreamt would have come his way. I learned a deep respect for one of Goethe's couplets: Whatever you can do or dream you can, begin it. Boldness has genius, power and magic in it! [6]

Murray's comments are certainly from the 'fortune favours the brave' school of thought, and his belief in providence – the guiding hand of a higher and beneficent power – suggests commitment and courage can induce unexpected good fortune. For what it's worth, I can add my own testimony to this belief; in both my own career and that of many of my clients I have regularly witnessed a number of 'chance' and beneficial circumstances arising - *in completely unforeseen ways* - once a firm intention and a definite effort had been made to achieve something.

However, whether these right place right time opportunities are gifted by some omnipresent, omniscient, and omnipotent intelligence, or whether these moments are simply random quirks of chance or coincidence, it makes sense to focus our attention on the critical factors of success that are *in our control.* By focusing our energy and resources on making our own opportunities and by developing a mind and skillset which allows us to capitalise on them, we can proactively shape our path to success.

Luck may bring us unforeseen opportunities,
perception and skill allow us to make
and take opportunities.

Should luck or the guiding hand of providence bring favourable circumstances to us - seemingly not of our making - we should be ready to take advantage but we shouldn't make these types of situations or coincidences the mainstay of our focus. It is for this reason that the concept of being in the right place at the right time goes beyond the idea of luck in the Inspired Movement model of success.

Redefining the right place right time phenomenon

In my experience, being in the right place at the right time is something high achievers work towards. They are not the sort of individuals to sit back and pray for good fortune. They do not wait for luck to dispense an opportunity; *they create their own opportunities.* Moving with perception, they are alive to the latent possibilities in *any given moment.*

The story behind the statue of David – a 17 foot marble masterpiece sculpted in exquisite detail by the renaissance artist Michelangelo – is a great example of this.

David is regarded as one of Michelangelo's finest pieces of work, not least because he carved it out of one large piece of marble that had been discarded by another artist and which had been left, exposed to the elements, in a church courtyard for over 25 years. Before Michelangelo was commissioned to work on it many artists at the time thought it was in useless condition. Michelangelo, however, *saw* a masterpiece hidden within in it and spent the next 2 years of his life bringing it out of the unwanted and unloved piece of marble.

Some might say Michelangelo was fortunate to have come across a piece of marble large enough to sculpt the statue of David but the truth is it lay untouched for 25 years because other artists decided to pass up the opportunity to work with it. When Michelangelo was shown the block of marble, however, he sensed it was the right time to work the opportunity *because* he possessed the artistic flair (the "optimal moves") through which he could transform it into a work of art.

The ability to see more in a situation, like Michelangelo, is a master skill that so many experts possess. Research has shown, for example, that chess masters can see superior moves on a chess board almost instantaneously compared to competent club players who require much longer to evaluate the same move. [7] Life, like chess, favours individuals who can see more in a situation. This ability to perceive greater possibilities, that others cannot see, is *the difference that makes the difference* in so many situations, especially in fast-moving environments where the ability to quickly capitalise on an opportunity can give a significant competitive advantage.

Inspired Movers see more in a situation.
They perceive moves that others can't see.

Take the FIFA 2013 Goal of Year, for example, scored by the Swedish Footballer Zlatan Ibrahimovic. The goal, scored in an international match against England in November 2012, was a moment of individual brilliance when, 30 yards out from goal, Ibrahimovic scored with a spectacular overhead kick. The sheer unexpectedness of the attempt caught all onlookers by surprise; no-one suspected that Ibrahimovic could see, let alone try and succeed with such an audacious attempt. After the game the England captain Steven Gerrard described it as, "The best goal I have seen live - an overhead kick from 30 yards when the ball is six feet in the air - only certain players can do that... he is a special player." Ibrahimovic was modest in his own appraisal of the goal: "When I saw the goalkeeper was out of his net, I tried to put it over him. It was a good try, and when it comes off it's fantastic." [8]

The ability to see the unexpected, as Ibrahimovic and Michelangelo did when expressing their respective artistic talents, is a key skill that also provides the competitive edge in the world of business, where investors look to get ahead of the market and entrepreneurs seek to gain a 'first mover' advantage over their rivals.

As we saw in the Fourth Master Move, Steve Jobs stole a march on his closest competitors by having the courage to launch products into the marketplace "completely unlike anything else in existence." Viewing life through his 'reality distortion field' Jobs perceived greater possibilities than others around him – and made those possibilities real for Apple and its customers.

George Soros – like Jobs – is another Inspired Mover who has shown a great ability to see and take advantage of latent opportunities. The 83 year old Hungarian investor – the 22nd richest person in the world and one of its richest hedge-fund managers with a net worth estimated at $20 billion [9] – is widely known for the financial alchemy he performed on Wednesday 16th September 1992: a day referred to in the history books as *Black Wednesday*; the day when the British Conservative government was forced to withdraw the pound from the European Exchange Rate Mechanism (ERM).

Unlike many politicians and market speculators at the time, Soros saw Black Wednesday coming, along with the resulting devaluation of the pound. Backing his own judgement and perception of events, Soros 'bet' $10 billion (more than the entire capital of his fund) on it happening; in essence Soros borrowed the equivalent amount in sterling in the UK and then re-invested the amount in the German Deutschmark. Following Black Wednesday, the value of sterling dropped by nearly twenty percent which meant Soros's fund made a profit of nearly a billion dollars – which in effect represented the surplus he was left with after he converted his Deutschmarks back into sterling and then paid off his now lower value sterling debt. This one single trade accounted for nearly 40 percent of his fund's profits for that year. [10]

Soros, Jobs, and Ibrahimovic – like Michelangelo – could see the potential value in their respective situations and were able to put into play the right moves to capitalise on an opportunity when it was presented to them. If, like these Inspired Movers, we wish to be alive to the latent possibilities around us, we must be open to the thought that *any given moment or situation* could be the right place and right time to act. It is for this reason that I define the right place and right time as:

Any **favourable moment** *in which we possess the moves that allow us to work the dynamics of that moment to our advantage.*

Within this definition, I use the word "advantage" to denote an opportunity to build towards our success and follow our Ideal Way Forward. Using this idea, we can potentially turn any moment into a *favourable moment* by asking ourselves: *What is the Ideal Way Forward in this moment?*

By repeatedly asking ourselves this question, and by sinking it into our subconscious minds (so that it can work silently yet actively in our habitual thought processes), we have the perfect mechanism to align ourselves - always - to the success that we desire most.

With this enhanced level of awareness, each and every moment then takes on a different level of meaning and our attention is more likely to remain focused – when it matters – on the *most opportune moment* of all which is always *right here and right now – the present moment;* the only moment in which we can ever make our moves. Using this definition we can now say that:

Greater success flows to those that can perceive, create, and capitalise on a greater number of favourable – right place right time – moments.

151

To demonstrate this idea, let's return to the sublimely gifted Roger Federer as an example. Federer is often described as an *'all court'* tennis player - he can serve and volley; he can rally from the baseline or come into the net when needed; he possesses a beautifully crafted backhand, a devastatingly powerful forehand and 'soft hands' which allow him to play exquisite drop shots should the opportunity present itself. Federer's all round game means there are a greater number of favourable moments open to him on a tennis court compared to less skilful players whose right place right time moments are restricted to fewer situations in which they can deploy their limited range of moves.

Even in difficult situations, where most other players find themselves in an unfavourable position, Federer's giftedness means that he can still potentially make these disadvantageous situations into favourable moments for himself. For instance, in the 2009 US Open semi-final match against Novak Djokovic, Roger Federer found himself in the precarious position of running at full pace to the back of the court (and away from the net) after he had been deftly lobbed by Djokovic. For most players in Federer's situation there would have been no shot to play, or move to make, or Ideal Way Forward to pursue in that moment. Federer, however, pulled off what one television commentator described as, "Not the shot of the match, not the shot of the tournament but perhaps the shot of the year." Unbelievably Federer hit a 'hot-dog' (through-the-legs) winner which left Djokovic looking stunned and rooted at the net as the ball whistled passed him.

Federer's hot-dog shot, like Ibrahimovic's overhead kick, or Soros's Black Wednesday bet, may have appeared at the time to be an audacious move, but each of these individuals *made* their respective situations into favourable moments because of the talent and resources they possessed. To less able individuals these types of moves are simply not an option. There is nothing of the sort on for them in similar situations.

---

*Greater skill allows Inspired Movers to work
situations to their advantage. At their best they
see favourable moments where others
see no such opportunity.*

The likes of Federer, Soros, and Ibrahimovic - like all other Inspired Movers in their respective fields - are thus able to *get more **out** of a situation by bringing more **to** it*. More often than not – in situations that matter to them – they perceive the optimal moves to make and have an ability to perform these moves with a sublime simplicity.

As Johann Sebastian Bach - the great 18th century German composer - said, "It's easy to play any musical instrument: all you have to do is touch the right key at the right time and the instrument will play itself." However, being able to strike the right note, hit the right shot, or make the right move, in each situation (especially when under immense pressure, as we shall see in the final Master Move) is far from easy. It requires us to cultivate what experts refer to as *situation awareness* [11] or what I described earlier as the *power of perception* - the ability in any given moment to make sense of what is happening around us and to discern what advantageous moves are open to us.

The Four Movers and the Power of Perception

We know now that Inspired Movers have a greater number of favourable moments open to them, at any given time in their respective fields, because they are able to combine the power of perception with an exceptional range of moves. In Figure 6.2, I have highlighted the relationship between these two dynamics. The four quadrants reveal what I refer to as the Four Types of Movers in any situation:

The Four Types of Movers

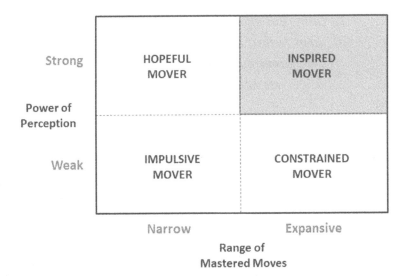

Figure 6.2

Impulsive Movers have no real grasp of the situation they find themselves in. They neither see many opportunities, nor do they possess many moves by which they could take advantage even if they could see them. There is little by way of forethought in the way they move. They simply act impulsively to events as they unfold around them.

Hopeful Movers can quickly make sense of what is happening around them, and are able to spot advantageous moves that are open to them, but their narrow range of mastered moves makes it difficult for them to capitalise to any great degree. Nevertheless these individuals may act on the favourable moments they see, but they move through hope rather than any degree of precision or skill.

Constrained Movers have an expansive range of mastered moves and can capitalise on favourable moments when they see them but they are constrained by their limited ability to see when and where they should make their moves. Constrained Movers are often talented individuals who have recently been immersed or exposed to faster moving or more dynamic situations (than they are used to) but who still need *time* to enhance their understanding of the events rapidly unfolding around them.

Inspired Movers, as we have seen, have an exceptional ability to understand what is happening around them and are able to perceive, create and capitalise on a greater number of favourable moments compared to the other three types of movers.

The power of perception combined with an expansive range of moves, increases the number of right place right time opportunities open to us.

These four types of Movers aren't necessarily classifications that are set in stone. They are instead situation-specific. It is possible, for example, that if we had reached a sporadically good, but not as yet exceptional, standard in our profession or passion, that we could conceivably have a few comfortable moments where we easily understand the dynamics of a situation and have the skill to work them like an Inspired Mover. But, likewise, we could find ourselves in more testing situations where we may act more like Hopeful or Constrained Movers.

Of all Four Movers, Impulsive Movers are at the biggest disadvantage because they are most at danger of being *deceived* in critical situations. The power of deception is definitely something that we must wise up to if we do not to want to be knocked off course in our desire to create success.

Deceptive tactics are commonplace in nature. For example the Margay, a small tree-dwelling cat that is found in Mexico, Central and South America, is able to mimic the calls of baby monkeys in distress. These calls attract the attention of anxious adult monkeys who go to investigate the calls but who are then attacked by the devious feline. Assassin bugs – another cunning species of nature – use deception to prey on spiders by mimicking the actions of distressed insects caught in webs. These bugs tap on a web's silk threads, in a way that replicates the vibrations of a fly or other insect.

The spider senses these vibrations and goes in to devour what it believes to be its own prey, only to be attacked and devoured itself by the deadly assassin bug.

Like animals and insects, humans also use deceptive tactics, and can deploy them in both playful and destructive ways. For example, deception (not to be confused with cheating) is a feature of many sports in which certain tactics or moves are used to dazzle, surprise or literally send opponents the wrong way. Deception is also used creatively in the entertainment industry. For example, the exceptionally clever movies *The Sixth Sense* and *The Usual Suspects* were built around story lines that intentionally set out to 'deceive' audiences until the very end of these films. I won't ruin the plots to these movies, in case you have not seen them.

The power of deception can, however, also be used fraudulently and deceitfully. For example, in 2009 the financier Bernie Madoff was given a 150 year prison sentence for masterminding an illegal $65 billion Ponzi scheme that deceived over 9,000 unfortunate investors who lost large sums of money, including the film directors Steven Spielberg and Pedro Almodovar, and the actors Kevin Bacon and Zsa Zsa Gabor. [12] Through the illegal scheme (named after Charles Ponzi who notoriously used the scheme in 1920) Madoff kept his clients' monies in a bank instead of investing it in stocks and shares and used money from new investors in the scheme to pay bogus returns to his clients, giving off the deceitful impression that the business was a successful and viable concern.

To avoid misreading situations that are important and relevant to us, or being deceived by clever opponents or fraudulent tricksters like Madoff, who can undo our attempts to progress in life, we need to sharpen our power of perception and see the true *causes* and *effects* of events happening around us. Moreover, to avoid working at a disadvantage and losing our competitive edge, we must have the definite aim of residing as much as possible in the top right quadrant of Figure 6.2: the realm of the Inspired Mover which is rich with favourable – right place right time – moments.

To help us achieve this aim, we now need to add to the practical knowledge of all the preceding Master Moves and learn how to see more in a situation.

Seeing more in a situation

Generally speaking, we generate an almost immediate subjective perception of any situation we find ourselves in. Neuroscientists suggest that the regions of our brains that support consciousness are updated between five to eight times a second. [13] However, to help us appreciate and understand the mechanics of this rapid perception, we can break down this key skill into three clear stages, which I refer to as:

- *Concentration* – the ability to pay attention to what is happening.

- *Comprehension* – the ability to understand what is happening.

- *Contemplation* – the ability to predict what might happen next.

Concentration is straightforward to explain: it involves holding our attention in a certain place or direction for as long as is desired. However, whilst it is easy to define - it is difficult to achieve. As we discussed in the last Master Move, we only have a limited capacity to pay attention (as it involves the slow and effortful System 2 mode of thinking). To demonstrate this point, the psychologists Christopher Chabris and Daniel Simons conducted an amusing experiment, which they described in their book *The Invisible Gorilla*. [14] The pair of them created a short video film of two teams (one wearing black shirts and the other white) passing a basketball to other members of their team. They then arranged for people to view the film and gave them one clear instruction: count the number of passes made by the white team only. Given the brisk movement of both teams the task required the viewers to pay close attention to what was happening. In fact, they were so absorbed by the task that a large number of them failed to notice that halfway through the film a person wearing a gorilla suit casually strolled through the scene and paused briefly for a second or two, for a spot of chest beating, before then moving out of view.

Chabris and Simons used their clever experiment to demonstrate the effects of "perceptual blindness":[15] a failure to notice some unexpected stimulus in our field of vision when our attention is completely absorbed by some task we are performing. The result of perceptual blindness is that paying attention to one thing comes at the potential cost of missing another entirely. This psychological limit on attention is likely to be one of the key factors that separates high performers from the rest. If we still have to think hard about how to perform our moves, our attention is tied up, and we are unable to look up and perceive more of what is happening around us. As Mica Endsley – one of the world's leading experts on situation awareness – pointed out:

So whereas it might be easy to consider the development of physical skills associated with task performance as separate from cognitive skills like SA (situation awareness), developing these physical skills to automaticity in order to off-load attentional demands may be an important prerequisite for developing high levels of SA. Expertise in SA may not be possible as long as an individual must concentrate on the performance of the physical tasks involved. [16]

As Endsley suggests, the degree of mastery of our moves and the degree of perception we have in a situation is linked. As we discussed in the last Master Move, Inspired Movers who have worked hard to make their moves as automatic and effortless as possible, are free to direct more of their attention to what is happening around them and are more likely to recognise and capitalise on favourable moments when they see them. If Federer had to think too hard about how to work his hot-dog shot, or Ibrahimovic had to concentrate on all the detailed mechanics of performing his overhead kick, or Soros had to work out from first principles how to execute his Black Wednesday currency trade, their *momentary opportunity* to take advantage of their respective situations would have vanished.

By making as many of our tried and tested moves as effortless as possible, we can then concentrate more effectively on developing situation awareness. We can begin to *comprehend* what is happening in any given moment and then *contemplate* what might happen as a result. It is then, and only then, that we can recognise favourable moments and capitalise on their latent possibilities.

*It is when we can effortlessly direct our moves
that we can then freely direct our attention to the
situation unfolding around us.*

In Chabris and Simons' perceptual blindness experiment, the person wearing the gorilla suit sauntered through a relatively calm situation in which six people moved around at a leisurely pace as they passed the basketball to each other.[17] Contrast this to, say, the fast moving situations that develop on a football pitch, where 22 players run at pace in rapidly changing patterns of movement. The ability to move with perception and to simultaneously concentrate, comprehend and contemplate such dynamic situations is a complex task. So coming back to Ibrahimovic's overhead kick against England, and his ability to have seen so much (and so quickly) in the seconds before he made his move: what exactly allows the best footballers in the world to see more in a situation?

The psychologist Norbert Hagemann, from the University of Kassel, and his colleagues who investigated the matter initially thought these players had a broader visual span that allowed them to see more of the pitch and the position of their team mates and opponents at any one time (compared to less able players). However, following their research project, Hagemann reported they were unable to find broader visual spans amongst better players. Instead, he discovered that higher performing players are able to pick up more information from a single glance by knowing *where* and *when* to look so that they can tune into the most relevant information. As Hagemann pointed out, they are more equipped to recognise and respond to *patterns* all over the pitch:

The less skilled player has to learn the structure of play, the patterns of the movements and so on. They have to build a knowledge base that helps them discover the relevant information in the current situation. If the best footballers already know what is going to happen then they will know where to direct their attention. Players like Messi are great at decision-making. They have anticipation abilities that help them solve complex problems in the best possible way. [18]

As Hagemann's research findings suggest, players like Lionel Messi are able to perceive more patterns of movement on a football pitch compared to less experienced or able players. These remembered patterns (or chunks) of information are stored in what psychologists refer to as 'mental models', [19] which can be rapidly accessed to make sense of what is happening and what is likely to happen in a situation.

When Messi runs with the ball at pace towards goal, his brain actively scans the scene before him and instantaneously runs it through his rich mental model of football. Messi is therefore able to decipher the position, body shape and movement of the opposition's defenders into recognisable patterns that he has seen (or are similar in some way to what he has seen) before. The result is that Messi can read the play and anticipate what moves are open to him.

Like Messi, Ibrahimovic's mental model of football has been comprehensively built-up through all the knowledge of the sport he has gained since he was a young boy. However, unlike Messi (who followed a structured development path since joining Barcelona's highly acclaimed youth academy as an 11 year old), Ibrahimovic learnt the game playing on the rough and tough streets of a Swedish town called Rosengard where he and his friends would try audacious moves, tricks, flicks and shots with a football. As Ibrahimovic told a BBC journalist, "When we played football in Rosengard, it was all about putting the ball between people's legs, doing different things. After every trick people were like 'oohhh' 'eeeyy'. It was all about who had the hardest shots, the best trick, the craziest move. I loved it." [20]

Ibrahimovic's mental model of football was therefore shaped by trying outrageous moves on the streets of Rosengard. For him, the crazy (six-foot off the ground) overhead kick was a real possibility in his concept of football despite it taking others completely by surprise. Ibrahimovic also added to his model (and created wider possibilities) by closely watching the Brazilian footballers Ronaldo and Ronaldinho and studying how they worked their moves. As he told the journalist, "I did not watch Sweden, I never watched Sweden. I loved Brazil because they were something different. They touched the ball differently, like field hockey where you drag the ball. That was magic and it felt totally different to anything I had seen before."

By closely observing his Brazilian role models, Ibrahimovic was able to perceive more, by tapping into a capability - that we all possess - of comprehending and contemplating how somebody else sees the world. However, as neuroscientists have suggested, this state of empathy goes beyond pure imagination; it arises, in part, from a special class of nerve cells in the brain called *mirror neurons.* [21] Remarkably these neurons don't just fire when we perform an action, but they also fire when we simply *observe* someone else performing the same action. Leading neuroscientists suggest that these neurons effectively allow us to 'read' others' intentions by running a mirror simulation of their actions through our own brains. Mirror neurons therefore set up the possibility of learning through imitation and through modelling other peoples' minds as well as their actions. [22] By closely observing the likes of Ronaldo and Ronaldinho, Ibrahimovic set up the possibility of tapping into their sublime mental models of football which, in turn, allowed him to expand his own.

The power of mental models

Mental models help explain how the Inspired Movers (that we covered in Part 1 of this book) were able to *read* important situations in their respective worlds. For example:

- Napoleon and Alexander the Great were highly experienced in the art of warfare and used their mental models of such situations to immediately make sense of chaotic scenes on a battlefield.

- Wayne Gretzky possessed a mental model of ice hockey that allowed him to "discern the game's underlying pattern and flow" and anticipate what would happen a little quicker and more reliably than anybody else.

- Zinedine Zidane had 'internal vision' or a mental model of the events on a football field which allowed him to see and take control of a game better than others.

Mental models, however, are not unique to any single group of people. We all naturally create them for situations we regularly find ourselves in, and they contain the knowledgebase we have acquired from past experiences and studies. This knowledge base is stored in our long-term memory and can be rapidly accessed so that we can quickly make sense of the world around us.

The information in these models helps us to recognise familiar patterns that allow us to predict what might happen next (by comparing what is happening now to what has happened before). If everything goes as we expect it (for example Federer or Ibrahimovic correctly anticipating the way a ball will behave after they have hit it) the patterns in these models become reinforced. However, whenever things don't go as we expect, or we are surprised by events, we are forced to pay closer attention and re-evaluate and recalibrate our mental models.

This means that the *quality* of our mental models are not all the same. As we discovered with the Third Master Move, Inspired Movers who love what they do possess a deep desire to know more about their passion. They are always expanding their horizons and taking in new information and experiences. And as we learnt in the Fourth and Fifth Master Moves, Inspired Movers have the courage, belief and confidence to build on what they know by continually seeking to master the next best move that is open to them. The result therefore of moving with passion, presence and precision is that Inspired Movers build broader mental models of their respective domains that are *richer, more complex* and *more accurate* than those of less committed or less able performers.

Richer mental models lead to a greater understanding of situations and an ability to better gauge what is happening now and what might happen next.

Greater knowledge, experience and awareness therefore translates into more powerful mental models that allow us to see through situations with greater clarity. As a result, some of us genuinely possess a more penetrating gaze through which we can better read people and circumstances.

For example, one of my clients – a CEO of a publicly quoted company – has a genuine ability to read people and has what some might refer to as a 'look that goes right through you'; a characteristic that is not without foundation.

As he once told me, "Whenever I speak to someone, I subconsciously focus on all the little details; what they say and do not say, how quickly or slowly they speak; the specific words they use and what they convey; the fleeting expressions that come and go on their faces; how they hold and express themselves; how well or not they present themselves etc."

Through years of interacting with people my client has built a rich mental model that allows him to better read individuals and their intentions. It is a skill which has been instrumental in helping him to select the right people to work with at the right time – a quality that has helped him to build and lead a thriving business. If, like this individual, we too desire greater success, and a greater flow of more favourable – right place right time – opportunities, we need to have the best mental models possible for the situations in life where we are required to make our moves.

Inspired Movers – and the most progressive individuals – are striving to get ahead by building the richest and most robust mental models they can. They are always seeking new information and new experiences and are happy to question 'what they know' to ensure their mental models are finely tuned and up-to-date.

Soros, for example, achieves this by following the principle of *fallibilism* – the philosophical idea that anything he believes may, in fact, be wrong and can therefore be questioned. [23] This personal philosophy ensures Soros always keeps an open mind to new information or developments which may disprove or improve upon a belief or position that he has previously held. It was because Soros was willing to question his own mental model, and that of conventional wisdom, that he was not *deceived* by the events of Black

Wednesday but was instead able to correctly *perceive* – and comprehend and contemplate - what would happen as a result. This greater perceptiveness presented Soros with a favourable moment that others couldn't see let alone profit from.

However, no matter how gifted we are, and no matter how rich our mental models become, it is important that we do not let them fall victim to what is colloquially known in academic circles as the *'toothbrush theory'* [24] : the idea that everybody needs a toothbrush, everyone has one, but no one wants to use anybody else's.

When we become deeply attached to our own mental models of a situation, and are unable to take on-board the views of others, we can potentially miss ways of expanding and refining our models by not consulting the views of those who *see life differently* to us or those who can (at present) *see more than us*. As Sir Isaac Newton said, "If I have seen further, it is by standing on the shoulder of giants." It is for this reason, that I always advise my clients (if they haven't done so already) to find the best mentor they can gain access to. Experienced mentors typically have a richer and deeper understanding of the domain or field in which we hope to succeed, and can greatly add to our mental models by filling in vital gaps in our understanding.

Regardless of whether they are starting out or whether they have years of experience behind them, many Inspired Movers invariably *seek out* a mentor that they trust, resonate with, and who they feel can help them go further in life. George Soros's ideas of fallibilism, for example, were heavily influenced by the philosopher and London School of Economics Professor Karl Popper - someone that Soros intentionally sought out. As Soros revealed, when he was in his final year at the London School of Economics, he could choose a tutor to study with; he decided to choose Popper after his book *The Open Society and Its Enemies* had made a deep impression on him. [25]

Likewise, Warren Buffet another heavyweight in the world of financial investment, sought out his mentor Benjamin Graham by similar means. As Buffet revealed in an article he wrote for Forbes, "Benjamin Graham had been my idol ever since I read his book *The Intelligent Investor*. I had wanted to go to Columbia Business School because he was a professor there, and after I got out of Columbia, returned to Omaha, and started selling securities, I didn't forget about him. Between 1951 and 1954, I made a pest of myself, sending him frequent securities ideas. Then I got a letter back: "Next time you're in New York, come and see me." [26] Graham then gave Buffet a job in his company, and although Buffet was only there for a short time (following Graham's retirement), it cemented a strong personal relationship between the two of them, that allowed Buffet to develop his highly regarded and successful 'value investing' model.

Another Inspired Mover, Simon Cowell – the producer of the highly successful TV show *X Factor* – revealed, in an excellent interview he gave to Emma Brockes (a feature writer for the Guardian), that he turned to his mentor, Sir Phillip Green – the billionaire British businessman – at a time when he felt overwhelmed by the pace of developments in his career and needed another perspective. As Cowell revealed, "What I was going through was just the inability to cope. I was trying to deal with everything – my business, the artists, the shows, everything – and didn't realise how difficult it was. He's incredibly well-meaning. And very kind. He became someone I could always go to. He makes you confront everything and find a solution." [27]

Some Inspired Movers are humble enough to turn to a mentor, even after having achieved great success in their own right. Roger Federer, for example, despite having won everything in the game of tennis and being widely regarded as its greatest ever player, recently employed the services of Stefan Edberg, a former world number one tennis player, to help him find a new dimension to his game. Despite being in its early days the Federer-Edberg partnership has helped Federer to experience a resurgent return to form (following a disappointing 2013) with the 17 times Grand Slam champion now playing a noticeably more aggressive style of tennis which has seen him more frequently move at pace from the back of the court to the net, to set up a greater number of clinical volley opportunities, and to tap into yet another stream of favourable – right place right time – moments for him to exploit and enjoy.

*Inspired Movers seek out perceptive mentors
wiser than themselves, who challenge, support and
help them to see further, wider, and deeper.*

However we expand our mental models – whether it's through greater experiences, more complex challenges, or through the eyes of someone wiser or more perceptive than us – it is vital work that we must undertake if we hope to see more in a situation and progress forward. Wherever we are in life, and at whatever stage in our journey, the ability to move with perception opens up further opportunities for us to work our way to bigger and better situations; situations that are infused with a greater number of right place right time possibilities on which we can build higher levels of success.

Applying the Sixth Master Move:

As the Sixth Master Move revealed:

- To enhance our understanding of success, we need to add the following questions to our Inspired Movement blueprint: *Where is the right place and when is the right time to make your moves?*

- Inspired Movers take the concept of being in the right place at the right time beyond the idea of luck.

- Within the Inspired Movement model of success, right place right time opportunities are defined as *favourable moments*. Any moment is a favourable moment *if* we possess the moves that allow us to work the dynamics of that moment to our advantage.

- Inspired Movers are able to *perceive* and get more out of a situation by bringing more to it - compared to either Impulsive, Hopeful, or Constrained Movers.

- The power of perception is defined as the ability - in any given moment - to make sense of what is happening around us and to discern what advantageous moves are open to us.

- It consists of three key elements. *Concentration* – the ability to pay attention to what is happening. *Comprehension* – the ability to understand what is happening. *Contemplation* – the ability to predict what might happen next.

- We create mental models that allow us to comprehend and contemplate situations by comparing them to patterns of information, behaviour, and movement that we have seen (or which are similar in some way to what we have experienced) before.

- These mental models allows us to predict what might happen next, by comparing what is happening now to what has happened before.

- Richer, more complex, and more accurate mental models allow Inspired Movers to perceive, create, and capitalise on a *greater* number of favourable – right place right time – moments.

The first step to enhancing your ability to move with perception is improving your power of *concentration*. Given that it is controlled by your System 2 mode of thinking, concentration requires effort to employ and build up. However the more you use your concentration the better it will function.

In general terms you can build up your concentration by keeping your attention focused on what it is that you're doing or observing, without getting distracted. To improve this skill, try a basic exercise like counting backwards from 100 down to 0 without getting distracted. If your mind wanders off at any stage, start again from 100 and repeat the exercise. If you find the exercise too easy start counting back from a bigger number like 300. If you find it too difficult, try closing your eyes and then visualising the numbers flashing up one after the other in your mind's eye as you count down.

To ensure you gain regular practice of doing this exercise, do it before your morning preview and evening review work, so that - in effect - you count down to these exercises. When you first begin doing this count-down practice you'll generally find that a multitude of other thoughts will attempt to *grab your attention*. But the more you persist and improve with it, the more you'll find you are able to *focus your attention at will*. As with all the exercises we've covered in applying each Master Move, do not be put off by its simplicity; its regular use will yield great results.

The next step in applying the Sixth Master Move is to improve your ability to *comprehend* important situations and see the genuine *causes and effects* of events unfolding around you. The evening review exercise that we have been working on since the very first Master Move will naturally help you to do this and will refine your mental model and understanding of situations.

At various stages of the book, we have added a number of progressive questions to the evening review exercise that we close each day with. To complete the set, add question 5 below to your list of evening review questions, so that in total they now comprise:

1. What worked today? What didn't work? What do I need to change?

2. What did I most love about my work or life today?

3. How bold was I today in expressing my Ideal Self?

4. Could I have achieved more with greater courage?

5. *Has anything I have learnt today changed my perspective in any way?*

To improve the final component of moving with perception – the ability to *contemplate* what might happen next in a situation and to anticipate any potentially favourable (right place right time) moments - use your morning preview exercise to imagine the important situations you will face in the day ahead. As you visualise these situations ask yourself: *What is likely to happen today? And what therefore is the Ideal Way Forward in these situations?* Then as you have become accustomed to doing so, visualise yourself as *precisely* and *vividly* as possible performing the optimal moves that allow you to best work these situations to your advantage.

However, do not stop there. Depending upon how important or critical a situation is to you (such as a big game or an important meeting or a major pitch), you can add to your visualisation of what is most likely to happen by asking yourself: *What would happen if.....?* This question allows you to then contemplate *multiple situations* that you may face in the day ahead and gives you the opportunity to see *ahead of time* what moves you may need to call upon if a situation demands it.

Bill Walsh – the legendary NFL coach of the San Francisco 49ers – gave an excellent demonstration of how to do this in his book *The Score Takes Care of Itself.* As we discussed in the last Master Move, Walsh revealed that his first twenty or twenty-five plays of a game would be scripted, along with a number of contingency plays. Walsh was able to contemplate his contingency plays by asking himself detailed *situational questions* such as: What if we fall behind by two or more touchdowns in the first quarter? What if specific key players get injured? What if weather conditions change? etc. [28] Asking *what if*, *what if, what if*, in a multitude of situations is an excellent way to enhance the predictive quality of your mental models.

To add to this work and to broaden your mental models even further, make use of the mirror neuron capability in your brain by *closely* observing how any Inspired Movers that you look up to, express themselves and their moves. As we discussed in this Master Move, your brain potentially has the capability to inwardly experience their actions and inner state. As Zlatan Ibrahimovic imagined what it would be like to move and play like his Brazilian football role models, *imagine if you were* the person who impresses and inspires you most in your life and work. In your practise or rehearsal sessions try to emulate this person's inner state and how they express themselves. Try and move, feel, and think as they do by using the whole weight of your imagination. After you have finished the exercise, ask yourself: *What is inspiring about the way this person sees the world, as I imagine it? Does this change my perspective or my Inspired Movement blueprint in any way?*

All these measures to improve your concentration, comprehension, and contemplation of important situations will, over time, greatly enhance the richness and quality of your mental models. However, as we discussed earlier in the chapter, it would also be highly advantageous to add to your knowledge by *seeking out* the best mentor you can find. You may or may not yet know this person, but it needs to be someone whose work you respect and who you feel can add a genuine dimension to your perspective. It is likely that these individuals will be exceptionally busy and will have great demands on their time but if you are serious about your success and can find a way to impress them with your passion, you stand a greater chance of them taking an interest in your personal journey.

If you're struggling to find someone to be your mentor, do not give up your search and take heart from W.H. Murray's belief in providence and in the old esoteric saying, *"When the student is ready the teacher shall appear."* As we shall see in the next and final Master Move, this element of having trust in yourself and in your journey is vitally important because when the time arrives to put all the talking to one side and to actually perform your moves, you will need to master the art of moving both *intelligently and intuitively* - without losing sight of who you are - if you hope to achieve the greatest success possible for you.

---

[1] Kipling, R., *Just So Stories*, (first published 1904), London, Walker Books, 2004.

[2] Smith, E., *Luck: What it Means and Why it Matters*, London, Bloomsbury, 2012.

[3] Gladwell, M., *Outliers*, London, Penguin, 2009, p19.

[4] Gladwell, M., *David and Goliath: Underdogs, Misfits and the Art of Battling Giants*, London, Allen Lane, 2013)

[5] Wiseman, R., *The Luck Factor*, London, Arrow, 2004.

[6] Murray, W.H., *The Scottish Himalayan Expedition*, London, Dent, 1951.

[7] Gobet. F., & Charness, N., *Expertise in Chess* in *The Cambridge Handbook of Expertise and Expert Performance*, eds. Ericson, K.A., Charness, N., Feltovich, P.J., and Hoffman, R.R., Cambridge, Cambridge University Press, 2006

[8] Ibrahimovic and Gerrard quoted in the online Daily Mail article, 15th November 2012: http://www.dailymail.co.uk/news/article-2233246/Zlatan-Ibrahimovic-scores-extraordinary-goal-wrap-crushing-4-2-win-Sweden-England.html

[9] See: www.forbes.com/profile/george-soros/

[10] Ferguson, N., *The Ascent of Money*, London, Penguin, 2009, p318

[11] Mica Endsley – the Chief Scientist of the United States Air Force and an internationally renowned expert on situation awareness describes it as: *"The perception of the elements in the environment within a volume of time and space, the comprehension of their meaning and the projection of their status in the near future"* see: Endsley, M.R., *Design and evaluation for situation*

awareness enhancement, In Proceedings of the Human Factors Society 32nd Annual Meeting, Human Factors Society, Santa Monica, CA: Human Factors and Ergonomics Society, 1988, pp 97-101.

[12] Teather, D., *Bernard Madoff receives maximum 150 year sentence,* The Guardian, 30 June, 2009.

[13] Cunningham, W., & Zelazo, P.D., *Attitudes and evaluations: A social cognitive neuroscience perspective,* Trends in Cognitive Sciences, 11: 97-104, 2007.

[14] Chabris, C., & Simons, D., *The Invisible Gorilla,* New York, Crown Publishers, 2010.

[15] Perceptual blindness is also referred to as "inattentional blindness".

[16] Endsley, M.R., *Expertise and Situation Awareness,* in *The Cambridge Handbook of Expertise and Expert Performance,* eds. Ericson, K.A., Charness, N., Feltovich, P.J., and Hoffman, R.R., Cambridge, Cambridge University Press, 2006.

[17] Chabris and Simons' Invisible Gorilla video can be seen online at: http://m.youtube.com/watch?v=vJG698U2Mvo

[18] Professor Hagemann's research and quotes are taken from a UEFA Champions League online Magazine, *Messi's sixth sense explained,* 7 February 2012: http://m.uefa.com/news/1749111/

[19] Mental Models have been defined in academic terms as, "Mechanisms whereby humans are able to generate descriptions of system purpose and form, explanations of system functioning and observed system states, and predictions of future states" – see Rouse, W.B., & Morris, N.M., *On looking into the black box: Prospects and limits in the search for mental models,* Atlanta, GA: Center for Man-Machine Systems Research, Georgia Institute of Technology, 1985.

[20] Smith, B., Zlatan Ibrahimovic: From teenage outcast to world great, BBC Sport website, 10 September 2013: http://www.bbc.co.uk/sport/0/football/24035146

[21] Mirror neurons were discovered by Italian researchers who first observed them operating in monkeys. See: Rizzolatti, G., & Craighero, L., *The mirror-neuron system,* Annual Review of Neuroscience 27: 169-72, 2004.

[22] Ramachandran, V.S., *The Tell-Tale Brain,* London, Windmill Books, 2011, p22-23.

[23] Soros, G., *Soros: General Theory of Reflexivity,* The Financial Times, 26 October 2009.

[24] The toothbrush theory explains what the psychologist Dan Ariely refers to as the *Not-Invented-Here bias* where people have the tendency to overvalue the usefulness and importance of their own ideas and theories and become, as a result, deeply attached to them. See: Ariely, D., *The Upside of Irrationality,* London, Harper, 2011, p117.

[25] Soros, G., *Soros: General Theory of Reflexivity,* The Financial Times, 26 October 2009.

[26] Buffet, W., *Warren Buffett's $50 Billion Decision,* featured in ForbesLife Magazine, April 2012. An online version of the article is available at: http://www.forbes.com/sites/randalllane/2012/03/26/warren-buffetts-50-billion-decision/
[27] Brockes, R., *Simon Cowell: Simon Says,* The Guardian, 23 September 2011. See online article at: http://www.theguardian.com/media/2011/sep/23/simon-cowell-interview-emma-brockes
[28] Walsh, B., *The Score Takes Care of Itself,* New York, Portfolio, 2009, p 54.

Master Move 7
Move with Poise

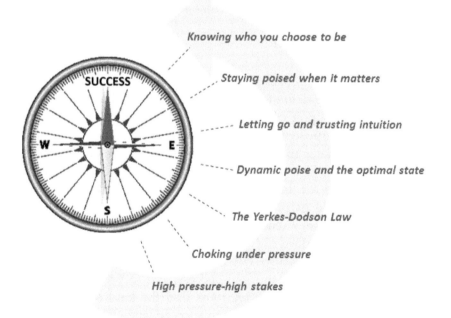

Knowing who you choose to be

Staying poised when it matters

Letting go and trusting intuition

Dynamic poise and the optimal state

The Yerkes-Dodson Law

Choking under pressure

High pressure-high stakes

When the time to perform is at hand, Inspired Movers remain secure in the knowledge of who they are and what they need to do. Letting go of the past and the future, they become dynamically poised in the present and remain open to what more they can become.

Cometh the hour

Everything we have covered on our journey together, has built progressively to this defining chapter and the last of the seven Master Moves. If you act upon what you have read and make a real attempt to pursue your purpose with passion and courage, you will inevitably arrive sooner or later to a defining point in your pursuit of success that I refer to as a high pressure-high stakes moment. These are the do or die, make or break moments in your journey that can significantly tip the balance between success and failure or victory and defeat. When a moment such as this arrives, the collective power of the six previous Master Moves stands us in great stead; but even now, after having come so far, it is important to take note that nothing is assured. To ensure our success, and to prevent ourselves being dethroned by pressure, we must find the kind of composure that helps the very best amongst us to succeed when it *really matters*.

Time and time again in life we find ourselves enthralled by high pressure-high stakes moments when the whole world seemingly stops still to bear witness to how men and women – courageous enough to put themselves in the firing line – stand up to the huge demands that are imposed upon them. These trying moments very often produce a unique intensity that brings out the very best in Inspired Movers.

For example, when, in August 1963, Martin Luther King uttered the immortal words, "I have a dream that my four little children will one day live in a nation where they will not be judged by the colour of their skin but by the content of their character," he did so in a highly charged atmosphere and in front of nearly a *quarter of a million people* who had come together at the Lincoln Memorial in Washington to hear his words. The speech itself came at a time when America found itself violently divided by its deeply unjust treatment of black Americans (just months before his speech, for instance, the country witnessed a low point in its history when black teenagers, who were marching peacefully in protest at segregation in Birmingham Alabama, were mercilessly knocked over in the streets by high pressure hoses wielded by white policemen, or were set upon by police dogs, or beaten with batons). [1]

Likewise, Winston Churchill's speech at the House of Commons on June 4 1940 – when he famously said, "…we shall fight on the seas and oceans, we shall fight with growing confidence and growing strength in the air, we shall defend our island, whatever the cost may be, we shall fight on the beaches, we shall fight on the landing grounds, we shall fight in the fields and in the streets, we shall fight in the hills; we shall never surrender" [2] – was delivered at a critical time in the second world war when victory or defeat was very much in the balance, and Churchill needed to rally the morale of his nation and the fighting spirit of Britain's weary troops.

When Churchill and King made their historic speeches the pressure on them to lead their people in the *right way* was immense as there was so much riding on their words. Churchill knew that if he failed to rouse his troops the Germans could realistically gain the ascendency in the war. King, on the other hand, had to be careful not to arouse the emotions of his followers too much; as he made his speech, the Pentagon had 19,000 troops on standby in case the peaceful protest at the Lincoln Memorial turned violent. [3] Both these inspirational leaders had to make the right moves when the eyes of the world were firmly and intensely focused on them - but how exactly did they manage it? And how do other Inspired Movers, like them, manage to compose themselves in high pressure-high stakes situations? To find the answer we need to begin by getting under the skin of pressure, and understanding the different ways in which it can affect us.

High pressure–high stakes

When it comes to our turn to 'face the music' or 'feel the heat', all of us respond in different ways. Some love the exhilaration of a high pressure – high stakes situation: they feel alive in the moment and they thrive under pressure. Usain Bolt, the fastest sprinter in the world, appears to love the minutes before a high profile race; many of his rivals, in contrast, look twitchy and nervous in the seconds before they go head-to-head. Indeed, Bolt is well known for play-acting with the crowd and having light-hearted fun with some of his fellow Jamaican sprinters. Speaking after winning gold for the 100 metres at the 2012 London Olympics, Bolt mentioned how he *enjoyed* the feeling of performing in front of the 80,000-capacity crowd in the London Olympic Stadium: "I knew it was going to be like this. There wasn't a doubt in my mind that it was going to be loud and it was going to be great. You can feel that energy, so I feel extremely good and I'm happy." [4]

When we see Bolt, and other men and women of a strong or relaxed disposition, looking calm in high pressure-high stakes situations, we may be led to believe that they are, in some way, immune to the negative effects of pressure or the weight of responsibility that has been placed on their shoulders. However, in my experience this is rarely the case – even the calmest and most mentally resilient of performers *feel the pressure*.

For example, some of the finest sports men and women have revealed how a high pressure-high stakes moment can play havoc with their emotions. Mark McCormack – the founder of IMG (one of the world's largest sports management agencies) – for instance once mentioned a revealing insight into the mental state of Bjorn Borg (considered by many to be one of the most composed sportsmen in history) in critical match situations: "Bjorn Borg had a reputation for being an iceman on the court. But he once told me that on key points he was always terrified, that sometimes it would take all the courage he could muster just to put the ball in play." [5]

Pelé – arguably the greatest footballer of all time and like Borg another sportsman of great composure – described how his emotions almost got the better of him when he was on the verge of scoring his 1,000[th] goal in football from the penalty spot: "I looked around and everyone was shouting *'Pelé!'* and my legs started shaking and I thought *'Oh my God! I can't miss this penalty. Please don't let me miss!'* Not even when I was 17 and playing in the 1958 World Cup, I wasn't trembling as I was when I went to score my 1,000[th] goal but thankfully the goal came." [6]

Victoria Pendleton, the British track cyclist, was equally candid when she revealed the emotional upheaval she felt in the moments before she won gold at the 2008 Beijing Olympics: "I was an emotional wreck beforehand because, while I was happy for everyone else, I was apprehensive about my ride. I worried that I would be the one person who let down the team. So winning was just a relief. And even that felt like a complete anti-climax." [7]

If we delve deeper into the history of Churchill and King we find that even these great leaders had moments when the pressure momentarily appeared too much. There were times, when the sheer scale of racial hatred in America, for instance, left King feeling despondent and upset when his choice of pursuing a conflict-free and patient approach to civil rights change appeared not to be working. [8] Likewise, Churchill too felt the effects of pressure and the weight of responsibility; a week before he gave his "We shall never surrender" House of Commons address, it is reported that he felt physically sick when he realised the Germans had swept their way to the Channel and that the Belgians had capitulated. [9]

When there is much at stake even the greatest Inspired Movers may become consumed by pressure.

The emotional state that Victoria Pendleton described, that Bjorn Borg and Pelé – two of the calmest of sportsmen – felt and that leaders as inspirational as Winston Churchill and Martin Luther King momentarily succumbed to, provides an indication of how many Inspired Movers find themselves frequently teetering on the edge of holding it all together when pressure threatens to overwhelm them.

Occasionally, however, it does and even the best of us can *choke* under pressure as the history of sport, in particular, bears testimony to.

For example, the 1994 World Cup Final saw Italy's most gifted footballer at the time, Roberto Baggio, step up to take Italy's fifth penalty in a shootout at the end of the game with Italy losing 3-2, only for him to unexpectedly blaze his spot kick high over the cross bar and hand Brazil the World Cup; the 1992 World Snooker Final saw the crowd favourite Jimmy White blow a 14-8 lead when he succumbed to pressure and lost ten consecutive frames to Stephen Hendry who eventually won 18-14; and the 1993 Ladies Wimbledon Tennis Final saw the unfortunate Jana Novotna fold under pressure when she was 4-1 up in the final set with a game point to make it 5-1, only to find herself double fault at the vital moment and then lose that and every game thereafter, handing her opponent Steffi Graff the Wimbledon title.

One of the most recent examples of choking in sport came at the 2012 British Open when the highly talented Australian golfer, Adam Scott, blew a four-shot lead with only four holes to play, thereby handing the Open Championship title to his rival Ernie Els. One journalist described Scott's fall from grace as:

There is no kind way to say it, but Scott could hardly have done a worse job. He bogeyed the last four holes in succession, compounding each mistake with another unrelated one — a blown sand save at 15, a missed 3-footer at 16, a wayward approach at 17, and finally, an errant drive at the last — until it resembled a chain-reaction car crash. [10]

After the match Scott looked as surprised as anyone by what had happened. He had no answers to explain why he had folded so dramatically under pressure. As he told journalists, "It's tough. You don't want to sit here and have to ... I can't justify anything that I've done out there. I didn't finish the tournament well today. But next time, I'm sure there will be a next time... I can do a better job of it."

As it happens there was a next time for Scott – he won his first ever Major Championship at the 2013 Masters. But, at the time of his infamous choking incident, he could find no reason to explain why he lost his way. There is, however, a possible explanation. The answer lies in a television game show and a revealing experiment conducted by psychologists.

The pressure game

The BAFTA award-winning British game show *The Cube*, has created an intriguing way of simulating the intensity of high pressure-high stakes situations. The game offers contestants the chance to win a top prize of £250,000 by completing a number of physical and mental challenges which are set within a 4m x 4m x 4m Perspex cube. The success and popularity of the gameshow is built squarely on a simple premise: even the most routine tasks become challenging when you are playing for big money in a confined space and in front of large studio audience.

Using slow-motion 360 degree filming techniques the show captures the emotional highs and lows of contestants, as they undertake progressively harder challenges for greater amounts of money. Each contestant starts out with nine lives and every time they successfully complete a task they move up the money ladder but should they make an unsuccessful attempt, they lose a life and have to repeat the game. Any contestant who runs out of lives whilst attempting a game is defeated by *The Cube* and leaves the show with no money. The show has been running since August 2009 and, to date, only one man has successfully managed to beat *The Cube*. Putting aside the natural fear of performing in public, why haven't more people managed to walk away with the £250,000 star prize?

The answer lies in an experiment researchers conducted into the psychological effects of excessive rewards.[11] Using residents of a rural Indian village as participants, the researchers gave each of them the opportunity to win a certain amount of money which was dependent upon how well they performed on six games (which tested their creativity, memory, and motor skills) and also on the classification of the reward bonus they would receive, which was randomly assigned; these bonuses were either 4, 40, or 400 Indian Rupees per game (being labelled low, mid, or high respectively) with the whole amount being paid out for what they defined as a "very good" performance level, 50 percent if they achieved a "good" performance level, and nothing if they failed to achieve this level. The dynamics of the experiment meant that if one of the participants was fortunate enough to be placed in the high-incentive group and was able to achieve a "very good" performance level in all six games he or she could win 2,400 rupees which equated to nearly half a year's average salary in the village and represented a substantial prize to the participants.

The result of the experiment was clear cut: participants who were 'lucky' enough to be placed in the high-incentive category (and could potentially win the most money) demonstrated the lowest level of performance. As the psychologist Dan Ariely – one of the main researchers in the experiment – pointed out, "The experience was so stressful to those in the very-large bonus condition that they choked under pressure." [12] The results of the experiment are very much in keeping with a well-documented finding in psychology which is known as the *Yerkes-Dodson law* – named after the psychologists Robert Yerkes and John Dodson who first proposed it in 1908. The law, as shown in Figure 7.1, states that performance (for complex or difficult tasks) increases with physiological and mental arousal but only up to a certain point at which it peaks (as shown at the apex of the inverted-U in the diagram – the point of optimal performance that I call *'dynamic poise'* (which we will explore shortly); however beyond this optimal point, our arousal or motivational levels become too high and our performance levels deteriorate. [13]

The Point of Optimal Performance & Inspired Movement

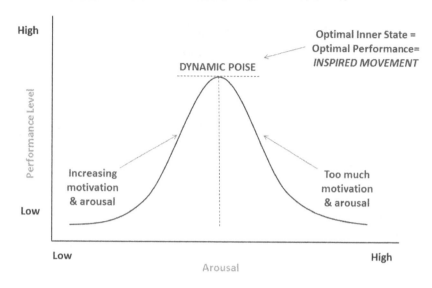

Figure 7.1

Whether or not the producers of *The Cube* were familiar with the Yerkes-Dodson law, I'm sure they would have intuitively known before they began filming the first ever show that the enticing prospect of winning £250,000 would create a state of over-arousal in most contestants (in exactly the same way as the opportunity to win 2,400 rupees did within the Indian villagers) leading most likely to a decline in their performance levels when they had the most at stake and *wanted to win too much*. In essence, only an exceptional individual, who is adept at handling pressure, can beat *The Cube*, as has proved to be the case! The only person to have successfully won the gameshow's £250,000 star prize (which was for charity in this case) was the runner and the 2012 double-Olympic champion, Mo Farah – a man who his coach described as someone with "more heart, more guts and more soul than any athlete I've ever seen." [14]

The Yerkes-Dodson law, therefore, helps to explain why the high profile sport stars, we mentioned earlier, choked under pressure: the stakes for winning were so high that their motivation and arousal levels quite possibly tipped over the edge. In other words, they may have *wanted it too much*.

---

*Desiring success too much can push the
success we desire beyond our reach.*

For example, when Baggio stepped up to take his penalty in the 1994
World Cup final, he had never won a World Cup before; when
Novotna faced up to Steffi Graff in the 1993 Wimbledon final she
had never won a Grand Slam title before; when Jimmy White played
Stephen Hendry in the 1992 World snooker final he had never won a
World Championship before (having lost twice previously and
eventually losing on all six occasions he reached the final); and when
Adam Scott lost to Ernie Els at the 2012 British Open he had never
won one of Golf's Major Championships before. Put another way,
neither Baggio, White, Novotna, nor Scott had won one of the top
prizes in their respective sports. When they found themselves
moments away from victory, their inner psychology and physiology
would possibly have told a revealing story of how they might have
lost their way...

Rising stakes that lead to a compromised state

As we learnt in the Fourth Master Move – *Move with Presence* – at the
point when we become motivated, engaged, and we believe we can
succeed in whatever we are doing, the brain releases a positive
cocktail of chemicals which boost our performance levels; in
particular, the reward chemical dopamine makes us feel more alive,
alert, and capable. As our motivation rises, so too does our dopamine
level and we feel increasingly sharper and on our game. There comes
a point, then, when our motivation and dopamine are at their optimal
level and we find ourselves *dynamically poised* in the best mental-
emotional-physical state to perform. The neuroscientist Ian
Robertson colloquially refers to this state as the *'Goldilocks Principle'*
referring to the point where our dopamine level is neither too much,

nor too little but is 'just right' (just as Goldilocks' wanted her porridge to not be too hot nor too cold in the classic fairy tale). [15]

When we reach this optimal state of dynamic poise *we feel fully alive and deeply connected and in control of what we are doing*; and we find ourselves performing at our effortless best, with a deep sense of enjoyment and with no distracting thoughts of adulation, failure or criticism. This optimal state of mind, and being, has been referred to with different names by different cultures. Within the fields of sport and business it is known as *being in the zone*. Within the creative or performing arts individuals talk of *being inspired*. The psychologist Mihaly Csikszentmihalyi famously described it as being in a state of *flow*. Zen Buddhists refer to it as *Satori*, meaning a deep sense of awakening or understanding. The Taoists refer to it as *Wei Wu Wei* which means 'effortless effort'. The Indian spiritual traditions refer to it as *Samadhi* which means at-one-ment – the experience of feeling at one with what we are doing. Regardless of what we call this optimum state, however, when we are poised within it we are able to tap into and trust some form of enhanced capability within us.

If, however, for some reason we lose our motivation and we become disinterested in what we are doing, our dopamine falls below the optimal level and we lose any semblance of energy, drive, or enthusiasm in our performance levels. On the other hand, if we want something too much, the reward-network in the brain produces too much dopamine which adversely affects the intricate workings and co-ordination of important brain regions causing our performance levels to suffer. [16] As we begin to feel less capable and in control of what we are doing, our anxiety levels rise and our bodies kick off the fight-or-flight (or stress) response which severely impacts our performance levels. Psychologists use terms such as 'flooding' or 'emotional hijacking' to describe what happens next: [17] our heart rates jump by 20 to 30 beats per minute in a single heartbeat, our main physiological systems – such as the muscular, respiratory and cardiovascular – can go into a temporary state of panic; we suddenly become survival rather than success-orientated; the capability of the executive centre of the brain (the pre-frontal cortex) becomes compromised as does the sophistication of our intelligence; as a result our thinking and decision-making become confused and we lose our ability to act with any real skill or subtlety.

183

---

*When we perform in an optimal inner
state we express the best of our talent.
When we compromise our inner state
we fail to do justice to our talent.*

---

*In short, when our inner state becomes compromised so too does our level of
performance.* We struggle then to even perform our tried-and-tested
moves with any degree of fluency. Instead of trusting the fast,
automatic, and effortless System 1 of thinking (that we referred to in
the Fifth Master Move) we flip control to the slower and more
cumbersome System 2, and the moves that we could perform
without any degree of thought or effort suddenly become complex
and unwieldy. We find ourselves thinking too much about what we
are doing and we become more prone to *perceptual blindness* as too
much of our attention is given over to how to perform our moves,
and too little is directed towards perceiving clearly what is happening
around us. The overriding effect of all these adverse changes is that
we begin to make the poor and erratic moves that are so synonymous
with the experience of choking.

The psychological and physiological effects of wanting it too much,
or conversely not wanting it all, make it clear that in order to perform
at our best and fulfil the sine qua non of Inspired Movement –
making the optimal move in the right place at the right time – we need to find
a way of staying dynamically poised in the optimal inner state, so that
when it matters most we are not weighed down by excessive pressure
nor carried away by high stakes.

Performing in high pressure-high stakes situations

When we see men and women of strong character remaining poised in high pressure-high stakes situations, we often hear the remark that they are able to *'hold their nerve'* when it matters most. This phrase is more than just a figure of speech; it refers to a genuine *physiological balance* that we need to achieve if we wish to perform at our best.

Human biology shows that, within us, there are two important strands to our nervous systems which are known as the *parasympathetic nervous system* (PNS) and the *sympathetic nervous system* (SNS). [18] The two intricate systems work hand-in-hand to govern our inner state and physiology. In essence, the SNS *fires us up* by activating the fight-or-flight response, whilst the PNS on the other hand helps to *calm us down* and find a steady inner state. If we consider the SNS to be the accelerator pedal of performance, the PNS is very much the brakes.

When we are able to find a state of equilibrium between these two branches of the nervous system, we discover the delicate point of balance - between too little and too much arousal and motivation - that defines dynamic poise. Leading scientists at the Institute of HeartMath in California refer to this optimal state as *psychophysiological coherence*. It is the point at which our mental, emotional, and physiological systems work with a high degree of *balance* and *synchronisation*. Or put in more simple terms, it is where the brain and the heart work in *harmony* with each other, enhancing our physical, emotional and mental performance. [19]

From a motivational point of view there is one of two ways of becoming dynamically poised. Depending on our character or temperament, and whether the SNS or PNS holds more sway in any particular moment, we either need to fire ourselves up or we need to cool ourselves down. For example, some performers perceive high pressure-high stakes moments as *do or die* situations; and they raise the pressure and ramp up the stakes by making the situation before them a matter of life or death. The traditional haka dance performed by New Zealand's All Blacks before a rugby match is a powerful demonstration of raising the emotional intensity of the moment. As the players perform the dance, and puff out their chests and slap their thighs, the leader of the dance shouts out *'Ka mata, ka mata'* *(I die, I die!)* whilst the team roar back *'Ka Ora, Ka Ora'* *(I live, I live!)*.

The retired sprinter and former 100 metres record holder, Maurice Greene, is another excellent example of someone with a do or die type mentality; before big races Greene used to visibly fire himself up by prowling on the start line like a hungry predator who was *poised* ready to devour his prey, which was in keeping with his source of inspiration – a motivational verse that he read to himself every day which said:

Every morning in Africa a gazelle wakes up. It knows it must run faster than the fastest lion or it will be killed. Every morning a lion wakes up and it knows it must run faster than the slowest gazelle or it will starve to death. It doesn't matter if you're a lion or a gazelle, when the sun comes up, you better be running. [20]

In contrast to Greene, and the do or die mentality, the world's current fastest man – Usain Bolt – (as mentioned before) approaches his big races in a completely relaxed frame of mind and prefers to play-act with the crowd rather than getting himself too worked up before running. Bolt's relaxed perspective allows him to deflect or enjoy the pressure that comes from being one of the world's most visible athletes. For example, when in the months before the 2012 London Olympic Games, Bolt learned that one million people alone had applied for tickets to watch the 100 metres final, he said, "When I heard that, it was just wow, wow, wow… This is going to be huge. Of course, it's going to make me a little bit nervous, but it's going to be fun. I like to make people happy, so the more people who want to watch me race, the better. I don't really get stressed." [21]

Like Bolt, other performers find a state of dynamic poise by *playing down* the stakes in big moments. As Matthew Syed revealed in his book *Bounce*, after he had choked in his opening table tennis match at the 2000 Olympic Games in Sydney, he ensured that whenever he competed thereafter he spent a few minutes playing down the significance of his matches by thinking about all the things that were more important than sport like his health, family and relationships; he would then finish his pre-match routine by telling himself: "It's only table tennis!". Syed devised this method with the support of his sport psychologist who described it as a form of *psychological manipulation* that alleviates the pressure in the vital minutes before it is time to perform by switching from a belief that winning or performing means everything, to one that suggests that it really doesn't matter. As Syed pointed out, Steve Davis – the six-time World Snooker Champion – captured the essence of this strategy by describing it as "the art of playing as if it means nothing when it means everything". [22]

Dynamic Poise is a state of inner balance.
It is the optimal point between too
much and too little motivation.

Regardless, however, of the nature of the stories we tell ourselves before we have to perform, they must lead us, in their own way, into the optimal state of mind; having let go of the past and the future and all thoughts of success or failure, we must become dynamically poised in the present moment - ready to perform our moves.

At this point, in the final few seconds before we thrust ourselves into action, some of us intuitively take a few slow deep breaths – which scientific findings suggest is a sound and important move. Research has shown that breathing deeply and smoothly for a few moments causes us to be both energised and relaxed at the same time as we rhythmically activate the SNS and PNS in turn, and bring them and our body-emotions-mind into an optimal state of balance. [23] It is then, once we are finally poised and ready to perform, that we are left with the *simplest and yet most difficult of tasks* – we need to let go and have faith in our ability to *move and think intuitively*.

The trust to let go and be in the moment

When we are dynamically poised in the optimal state and we are performing at our effortless best, we find ourselves in a *paradoxical* position: we feel in complete control of what we are doing and yet we feel as though we are not thinking or directing our actions at all.

It feels, instead, that we are *intuitively* guided by some greater power. For example, when the psychologist Mihaly Csikszentmihalyi interviewed many leading professionals in his research into the flow experience, many spoke of it in such terms; the physicist and author Freeman Dyson described it as, "...when I am writing it is really the fingers that are doing it not the brain. Somehow the writing takes charge." The novelist Richard Stern suggests that, "At your best you're not thinking." [24]

Phil Jackson, one of the greatest coaches in NBA history, described top-level basketball as intuitive movement when he said, "Basketball is a sport that involves the subtle interweaving of players at full speed to the point where they are thinking and moving as one. To do that successfully, they need to trust each other on a deep level and know instinctively how their teammates will respond in pressure situations." [25]

Likewise, in his translation of Lao Tzu's classic book *Tao Te Ching* (The Book of the Way), the author Stephen Mitchell described the intuitive nature of Wei Wu Wei (effortless-effort) as: "A state of body-awareness in which the right stroke or the right movement happens all by itself, effortlessly, without any interference of the conscious will... The game plays the game; the poem writes the poem; we can't tell the dancer from the dance." [26]

To remain poised in this sublime state, we must have a deep trust in our intuition and greater *'unconscious'* capability. Consciously letting go, however, of our desire to completely control a situation is something many of us find difficult. Performing at our best, and trusting our intuition, requires us to find what can be an elusive and delicate balance between control and instinct, between thought and feeling, and between the head and the heart. It is this balance that Bruce Lee's quote from part one of the book alluded to, in which he said: "Here is natural instinct and here is control. You are to combine the two in harmony... If you have one to the extreme you'll be *very unscientific*. If you have another to the extreme you become all of a sudden a *mechanical man*, no longer a human being."

Having been born in England but raised in a Sikh family I know that, generally speaking, there is a greater acceptance and trust of intuition in Eastern traditions but a greater scepticism of it in the West, where there is a preference for rational intelligence and conscious control.

This *'Western scepticism'* stems from the fact that thinking and moving intuitively seems paradoxical. When we act through intuition we may know something without knowing *how*, or *why*, we know it or we may effortlessly perform complex moves without *consciously* thinking about how we are orchestrating them.

However, some of the brightest minds in history swear testimony to its powers including Aristotle, Spinoza, Michael Faraday, William James, Carl Jung, Bertrand Russell, Jonas Salk, and Albert Einstein [27] who famously said, "The only really valuable thing is intuition." Furthermore, there has been a growing interest in intuition in academic literature as recent discoveries in neuroscience and psychology illustrate that much of our cognitive processes occur outside our everyday conscious minds. For example, as we learnt in the Fifth Master Move, scientists suggest that the unconscious mind can apparently process 11 million bits of information per second whilst the conscious mind can manage only 40. [28]

When we stop to reflect, we do not need to think too hard to realise how capable our unconscious capability actually is; the vast intelligence that runs the intricate and highly complex processes of the human body, for example, operates without any conscious thought on our part – the human brain being a good case in point. As we know from an earlier chapter, it contains approximately 100 billion nerve cells or neurons, each of which can make somewhere between a 1,000 to 10,000 connections with other neurons. As one neuroscientist suggests, this huge population of interacting units (which are in a constant state of flux) could potentially lead to immense noise and chaos, and yet the brain rapidly assumes highly ordered and synchronous states. [29] On a conscious level we have no idea at all about how the brain performs such complex moves, as we go about making moves of our own.

Some scepticism of intuition persists because many refer to it as a vague heart-felt, gut-felt (or simply some other instinctive) feeling that guides us to make certain moves. For example, as the late Steve Jobs said, "....have the courage to follow your heart and intuition. They somehow already know what you truly want to become. Everything else is secondary." However, research shows that even our intuitive feelings have a scientific basis and that the heart does appear to play a central role in intuition.

Scientific findings suggest that the human heart has a great degree of power and sophistication in its own right; in fact Institute of HeartMath scientists have discovered that the heart is the most powerful generator of electromagnetic energy in the human body (even more so than the brain).[30] However, the really intriguing finding that their research has uncovered is that gentle and rhythmic breathing, whilst focusing our attention on the heart area and simultaneously recalling a positive *feeling* to mind, results in our heart-rhythms becoming more coherent – inducing the optimal state they referred to as psychophysiological coherence (or heart-brain harmony) – which they suggest, based on their findings, helps to create a heightened state of intuitive perception within us.[31] It seems true, therefore, that access to our fullest capability, really does depend on the heart and head functioning with equal power.

Interest and credibility in intuition has also grown as recent scientific discoveries point to our ability to learn implicitly. In other words every day and through every experience we tacitly (or silently) acquire greater knowledge without consciously being aware of it. The psychologist Daniel Goleman, a pioneer in the field of emotional intelligence, explained why access to this silent knowledge comes in the form of *intuitive feelings* in his book *The New Leaders*:

Because this kind of learning goes on largely in a deep zone of the brain outside of the reach of words (in the basal ganglia, a primitive part of the brain atop the spinal cord), leaders need to trust their intuitive sense to access their life wisdom. The circuitry involved in puzzling decisions, in fact, includes not just the basal ganglia, but also the amygdala, where the brain stores the emotions associated with memories. When it comes to drawing on a lifetime of silent learning… it's not the verbal part of the brain that delivers the best course of action – it's the part that wields our feelings.[32]

The form of intuition that Goleman describes is often referred to as *expert-intuition;*[33] experienced performers use this intuition to draw upon their accumulated wisdom and to support their decision making in fast moving or complex situations. In such situations, the time-consuming process of rational analysis is not feasible, and quick moves and decisive decisions are a necessity. In such situations expert-intuition appears to actually *enhance* our decision-making capability; research studies have shown, for example, that the intuitive first move or course of action proposed by expert performers is often of a significantly high quality [34] and that intuitive decision making can result in higher performance than analytical processes. [35]

Other research studies demonstrate that senior business executives, for example, make significant use of expert-intuition when there is simply too much information or complexity to process within the tight timescales in which they operate. A senior executive from one of the world's largest pharmaceutical companies, cited in one research study, describes how expert-intuition becomes necessary as you move up the career ladder: "Very often people will do a brilliant job up through the middle-management levels where it's heavily quantitative, in terms of decision making. But then they reach senior management, where the problems get more complex and ambiguous, we discover that their judgment or intuition is not what it should be. And when that happens, it's a big problem." [36]

The former US President Bill Clinton echoed this view when he said, "I think intellect is a good thing unless it paralyses your ability to make decisions because you see too much complexity. Presidents need to have what I would call a synthesising intelligence." [37]

As Clinton suggests, expert-intuition is needed when we cannot afford to succumb to *paralysis by analysis;* this helps to explain why a study into the split-second decisions taken by fire-fighters in high pressure-high stakes situations, found that 80 percent of their decisions were based on rapid and unconscious assessments, in which they intuitively recognised the dynamics or patterns of a situation based on their experience.[38] This form of expert split-second decision making works in much the same way that top sports professionals are able to intuitively read the patterns of play in their respective sports and then decipher what move to make next (as we discovered in the last Master Move).

However, whilst we can find a rational basis to explain intuition and galvanise our faith in it, keeping ourselves dynamically poised in this optimal, intuitive, and enhanced state of mind, is one of the greatest challenges facing all of us who wish to perform at the highest level.

There is a greater capability within us. We access
it when we let go and trust our ability to think
and move intuitively.

Letting go and trusting our greater inner capability is difficult when our minds are prone to thinking too much and negative thoughts frequently rob us of the relaxed and quiet state of mind that acts as gateway into the optimal inner state. Keeping our composure in high pressure-high stakes situations is no easy task, when our hearts and minds race ahead with the exciting prospect of success or the debilitating fear of failure. As the old saying goes, "Anyone can hold the helm when the seas are calm" – *real character* and *heart* reveal themselves when the pressure to perform is at its most intense.

When the Ideal Way Forward is a narrow razor edged path, in which there is a very thin line between victory and defeat, or success and failure, we need to somehow find the equanimity and strength of character that Kipling described so poignantly in his poem *If*:

If you can dream – and not make dreams your master;

If you can think – and not make thoughts your aim;

If you can meet with Triumph and Disaster

And treat those two imposters just the same;

…Yours is the Earth and everything that's in it,

And – which is more – you'll be a Man, my son!

If we are to let go and trust in ourselves when it really matters, and if we are to be truly poised in a position of strength and power – when the stakes and the pressure are high – there are two essential requirements that must be met. What is more we must add the last of

192

Kipling's six honest men (from the previous Master Move) – 'who' – to our Inspired Movement blueprint, so that it is complete.

The defining 'who' of Inspired Movement

The first essential requirement of letting go and trusting ourselves, is that we must be *secure in the knowledge that we possess the moves that will allow us to succeed.* As we spoke of in the Fifth Master Move – Move with Precision – we must map and master the moves of success if we are to steady our emotions and perform with any degree of genuine confidence and self-assurance. As we mentioned in that chapter, Jonny Wilkinson *knew* he could succeed by using his tried and tested routine of mentally returning to the training ground and then visualising himself kicking the rugby ball in the way he had done thousands and thousands of times before. As Wilkinson openly revealed at the height of his international rugby career:

The responsibility as England's kicker does scare me. I worry all the time about it, but the important thing is that I know I can worry about it. ... As long as when I go to take the kick, my routine is there, and my visualisation, I can be as fearful as I like and think: 'I'm really, really concerned about this.' But as long as everything is in place, the ball will go where you want it to. [39]

Of this first essential condition we need not speak any more as we have covered, at many points throughout this book, how Inspired Movers work hard to perfect their moves. However, as this book draws to a close and our journey together reaches an end, I would like to finish by turning our attention to the second essential condition that we must fulfil if we are to let go and truly trust ourselves when it really matters – *we must be secure in the knowledge of who we are and the values we stand for.* It is here that we return back to the high pressure-high stakes situations that we opened this chapter with; situations that faced the great leaders Martin Luther King and Winston Churchill. In my opinion, King and Churchill were able to hold their nerve and perform in the intense and volatile situations that they found themselves in, because they knew who they were and what they stood for.

When King had to address the huge crowd that gathered at the Lincoln Memorial in Washington in August 1963 he did so *poised in the moment* with a very clear idea of *who he was*. History shows that King was a deeply religious man who stood for justice, freedom, and equality for all people. King was able to find the right tone in his speech because he was grounded in his deeply Christian values and used them to appeal to both the white and black population of his country. As Howard Gardner, the Harvard professor, described in his book *Leading Minds:*

King was knowledgeable about the Bible, the life of Christ, the prophets and the saints, and the more theological texts. He identified profoundly with the Christian tradition, with the stories of the Old and New Testaments, and particularly with Christ, whom he called the most influential person who had ever lived... King had been raised in the church and felt its spirit coursing through his body. The church was his natural pulpit, the congregation his natural audience. Even when he addressed other populations in secular settings, the minister was never far from the surface. [40]

In fact, King was so clear in who and what he represented that he was prepared to sacrifice everything for it; as he once told a reporter, "Once you become dedicated to a cause, personal security is not the goal. What will happen to you personally does not matter. My cause, my race, is worth dying for." [41]

Like King, Churchill knew who he was and what he stood for when he gave his "we shall not surrender" speech at the House of Commons on June 4 1940. Churchill was an indomitable leader, whose defiant words helped his nation find inner strength and resolve when it was most needed. For instance, when some members of parliament suggested that the royal family should be evacuated to a safe and distant location somewhere in the British Empire, Churchill said, "No such discussions are to be permitted," and when someone else suggested the most important art pieces in the National Gallery's collection should be shipped to Canada, Churchill said, "No. Bury them in caves and cellars. None must go. We are going to beat them." [42]

When King and Churchill were tested in their respective high pressure-high stakes situations, they were successful because they possessed the *unshakable poise* that only comes when we authentically embody who we are and we remain true to what we stand for.

In testing times we can remain poised in a position of strength, when we are secure in the knowledge of who we are, what we stand for, and of the moves we possess.

Like King and Churchill, many of the great Inspired Movers that we have come across in this book made *a definite choice* at some point or other to be who they are. *Every move they subsequently made was defined by this principle decision.*

In the year after King made his speech, for example, another greater leader, Nelson Mandela, was equally unequivocal about what he stood for, when he was on trial in April 1964 before the supreme court of South Africa on charges of sabotage. At the time he said, "I have cherished the ideal of a democratic and free society in which all persons live together in harmony and with equal opportunities. It is an ideal which I hope to live for and to achieve. But if needs be, it is an ideal for which I am prepared to die." [43]

Mandela lost more than 27 years of his life in prison standing up for his ideal, however, as we learnt from the Fourth Master Move, he *chose to be optimistic* in his darkest moments and that optimism helped him to make the right moves in leading his people. Likewise, we also discovered that Mahatma Gandhi *chose to be peaceful* in the face of a violent and unjust occupation of his homeland - a move which helped him to free his people from British rule and give them back the land and tradition that rightly belonged to them.

As we have learnt in our Inspired Movement journey together, like Churchill, King, Mandela and Gandhi, many of the greatest movers and thinkers of our time, from many different fields and backgrounds, made the choice to be who they are; J.K Rowling *chose to be imaginative* when others thought her imagination wouldn't pay the bills, a decision which led eventually to her becoming a successful author when she stopped pretending to herself that she was anything other than who she was, and she began to direct all of her energy into finishing the only work that mattered to her. The actor Will Smith *chose to be more hardworking* than anyone else in his field in his bid to be successful. The actor Bruce Lee simply *chose to be like water* when he expressed his martial arts. The billionaire investor Warren Buffet's considerable success came after he *chose to be patient and thorough* when investing. The great technology entrepreneur Steve Jobs *chose to be visionary* when building an iconic business that brought to the world products it had never seen before. When we look back on the career of the great Usain Bolt, we will see a man who *chose to be an entertainer* as well as the fastest man in the world. The all-conquering Barcelona team of 2010-2011, that comprehensively outplayed Manchester United in the Champions League Final, did so as its players *chose to be selfless* in giving the ball to the right player at the right time in the right place. Likewise, one of the greatest basketball players of all time, Michael Jordan, helped his teammates to secure three consecutive NBA championships after he matured into a consummate professional that *chose to be a selfless multidimensional player* that worked tirelessly for the good of the team.

The act of choosing to be who we are is one of the greatest decisions we can make in our journey through life. This one decision defines us. It gives us our unique identity and self-expression. It is what determines whether we choose to play the game of life like a warrior or an artist, or whether we choose to create our success by moving with power or grace. In fact, this one defining act, is so essential to Inspired Movement, that we must add the all-important question – *who do you choose to be?* – to the very head of our Inspired Movement blueprint (see Figure 7.2) and in doing so, finally make use of the last of Kipling's six honest men.

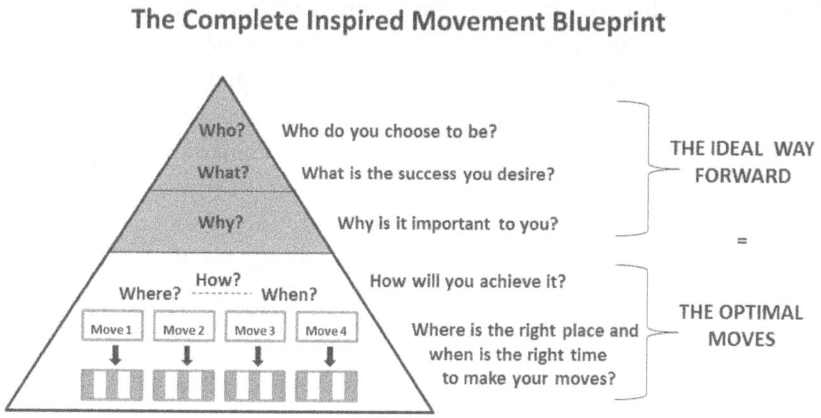

The Complete Inspired Movement Blueprint

Figure 7.2

If we can know with great confidence and certainty *who we choose to be* and we can make the courageous decision to *be this way*, time and time again, we stand a greater chance of being poised and centred when we come face-to-face with the key high pressure-high stakes moments in our lives and careers. There is no hesitation or second guessing as to how we should respond in any such situations. We simply act in the way that feels most natural to us and most true to the values that resonate inside of us. Every time we make a choice to live our life *in complete alignment* with this vision of ourselves we shape our personality in *definite* and *desired* ways; we build a cumulative force of character; we create a *predominant* way of thinking, feeling and acting that allows us to let go and make our moves decisively, convincingly, and intuitively in the moment.

The moves we repeatedly make define us.
By choosing to be who we are and by
staying true to the values that represent
us, we build an unshakable poise that
becomes a definite part of us.

By knowing who we choose to be – our *Ideal Self* – and by knowing how to create the success we desire – *the optimal moves* – we find ourselves poised and ready to move in a way that most represents our *Ideal Way Forward*. Then, *who we are is expressed through what we do*. We are then able to truly let go and enjoy the exhilarating experience of *discovering more of who we are,* that the great Formula One driver, Ayrton Senna, once described when he said, "The harder I push, the more I find within myself. I am always looking for the next step, a different world to go into, areas where I have not been before... That is my excitement, my motivation."[44]

When we let go and are dynamically poised in this way – deeply connected to what we are doing and who we are being – we discover a latent source of *greater* strength and capability within us; a source that allows us to do more and be more. We then find ourselves *progressing* into a higher dimension in which our *passion* is heightened and our *purpose* is furthered; it is then that we grow in *presence* and we can *perceive* more and act with greater freedom and *precision*; it is then that our *poise* becomes unshakeable; and it is then that everything comes together – and all the Master Moves combine – to unleash the full power of *Inspired Movement*.

Applying the Seventh Master Move:

In the Seventh Master Move we discovered that:

- There is an optimal inner state of *dynamic poise* that leads to an *optimal level of performance.*

- This state occurs when our motivation level is just right. In this optimal state our head and heart and mind and emotions function with equal power and *we feel fully alive and deeply connected and in control of what we are doing and who we are being.*

- If our motivation is either too little or too much, our inner state and our performance level becomes *compromised.*

- When we are dynamically poised, we can let go and trust ourselves to think and move intuitively in the moment, and we can *enhance* our decision-making by tapping into the greater (unconscious) capability within us.

198

- *Expert-intuition* may manifest as a feeling or a sense of knowing without us knowing how or why we know; but through it we are able to access our accumulated knowledge, experience and wisdom that we have acquired either tacitly or actively through years of dedication to our work.

- Unshakeable poise and deep trust in our inner capabilities comes when *we are secure in the knowledge that we possess the moves that will allow us to succeed, and we are secure in the knowledge of who we are and the values we stand for.*

- The act of choosing who to be is one of the greatest and most defining decisions we can make. Our truest moves and most authentic self-expression flows from it.

As you'll have become aware through applying each Master Move, the practical exercises that support Inspired Movement are centred around the morning preview and evening review exercises which are to be performed *each* and *every* day, along with the vitally important work of mapping, chunking, and physically mastering the moves that will create the success you desire.

Now that you have reached the end of the book, take the opportunity to re-read the *'Applying the Master Move'* sections at the end of each chapter and familiarise yourself more deeply with the practical and theoretical elements of each Master Move.

Know that the practical component to the Inspired Movement model of performance is *essential* if you are *serious* about creating the success you desire. By making a concerted, regular, and genuine attempt to undertake these practices you will stand a greater chance of consolidating the *transformational changes* that will create a *dynamic shift in your performance.*

To apply the Seventh Master Move, practice entering a state of dynamic poise before your morning preview and evening review work. To do this, begin these sessions with 15 minutes of breathing consciously, gently, and smoothly. As we learnt in this chapter, this causes you to be both energised and relaxed at the same time by bringing your nervous system and your heart and brain into a state of balance.

Spend the first 10 minutes of this breathing practice by focusing on nothing other than your breath flowing in and out of your body. Ensure each inhalation and exhalation is a *complete breath*. This can be achieved by breathing into and expanding the abdomen and then the lower, middle and upper chest in turn. With the abdomen slightly drawn inwards, hold the breath for a few seconds, and then breathe out the air in the lower abdomen first and then from the lower, middle and upper chest in turn. If any thoughts distract you, and your mind wanders during this practice, gently bring your attention back to where you are and focus on your breathing once again.

In the final five minutes, however, finish with the exercise we covered in the Fourth Master Move that enhances your feeling of inner presence. Imagine you are somewhere where you feel inspired or somewhere that gives you a feeling of strength. Reside in this inner space for a few minutes and imagine yourself drawing in the strength and inspiration from your surroundings. Tell yourself that this space you have created within yourself is free from all doubt and negativity. Feel your presence and sense of self expand with this thought and then let go of the scene but make an attempt to retain the inner feeling of strength.

Alternatively, spend these five minutes recalling a time when you felt in a strong and positive state of mind. Remember that experience as vividly as you can. Reconnect with how you felt and bring that feeling to mind with greater intensity with each breath. Let it infuse into your whole body. Feel as though you are in touch with the greater capability within you.

As we discussed in the Fourth Master Move, it does not matter whether you perceive this greater capability to be a higher or metaphysical power or an optimal psychological and physiological state; it is important, however, to use your imagination – in a way that feels natural and in accordance with your beliefs – to feel yourself enter and be poised within an *enhanced* and *expansive* state of mind and being.

If you suffer from a medical condition seek advice from your doctor before introducing this breathing practice into your morning and evening schedule. Most importantly, do not strain or inhale or exhale or hold your breath for longer than is comfortable. If you can, use your breathing practice to create a state of *attention without tension*.

Ensure your spine is always erect and self-supported and that your head is neither titled forwards nor backwards and check for any tension in your face, shoulders, or any other part of your body. If you feel any stiffness in your muscles, momentarily contract them as you breathe in and hold for four to five seconds before consciously breathing out and letting go of the tension. Repeat this cycle until you feel a softening of these tense muscles. Breathing and relaxing your muscles in this way will activate the calming component of your nervous system (the PNS) and avoid your brain firing off the fight-or-flight response unnecessarily.

As you add this breathing practice into your daily schedule, you will find yourself carrying this poised and attentive state of mind into the day. However, consciously make a habit of taking a few complete breaths, whenever opportunity presents itself, or in your quieter moments to reconnect and rebalance your body and mind.

The more you do this practice the greater the results it will yield. Neurological research has shown that people who practice mindfulness for as little as an eight-week period feel less stressed, more creative, and have a greater feeling of enthusiasm for their work; moreover, research shows that an observable shift takes place within our brains with less activity occurring in the right prefrontal areas (which are associated with creating negative emotions) and more activity generated in the left prefrontal area where positive and optimistic emotions are generated. [45]

Whenever you engage in these moments of mindful breathing, use the time to *tune into your inner state* by asking yourself: *What am I thinking?* and *What am I feeling?*

This will enable you to become more sensitive to your thoughts, emotions, and any intuitive feelings within you. This ability to 'tune-in' is especially important in the moments leading up to a high pressure-high stakes situation.

The ability to tune into your emotional state is often referred to as the ABC model of emotions. [46] 'A' represents the situation – what is actually taking place. 'B' represents how you interpret the situation – the story that runs through your mind of what is happening in the situation. 'C' represents your reaction and emotions to your story or interpretation of events. As we discussed in this Master Move, the story we tell ourselves in the moments before we have to perform may either fire us up or cool us down depending on our temperament. By tuning into your inner state you can become aware of the story being played out in your mind. *If the story doesn't serve your purpose, choose one that resonates more positively with you and which puts you in the optimal frame of mind to perform.*

This last step, however, is often easier said than done. Many thoughts will race through your mind in the days, hours, minutes or seconds before you have to step up and perform on a big occasion that has much riding on it. However, in my experience, it is the *predominant story* – the one that carries the most weight in your mind – that will win out and influence how you think, feel, and act.

This predominant story is shaped by the moves you have made time and time again and thoughts and feelings that you have allowed to dominate your inner world in the past. The central character of this story is who (deep down) you believe you are. To ensure you take control of your own story and shape your character in definite and desired ways, you must decide *unequivocally* who you choose to be – your *Ideal Self* – and then live and breathe in complete alignment with this vision of yourself. By doing this you will create a predominant way of thinking, feeling, and acting that represents the *best of who you are.*

To do this, revisit the important work you began, in applying the Fourth Master Move, of constructing your Ideal Self. Ask your yourself the question: *'Who do I chose to be?'* In answering the question, state what three values most define you. Regularly affirm these qualities to yourself by using the affirmation *'I am....'* and then stating your three defining values. For example, you may say to yourself, *'I am creative, artistic, and graceful'* or *'I am dynamic, decisive, and powerful'* or *'I am dependable, honest, and hardworking'.* Keep this defining affirmation at the forefront of your mind, repeat it to yourself often (especially when you have entered a state of dynamic poise). Most importantly, add the question *Who do I choose to be?* and your three defining values at the head of your *Inspired Movement blueprint for success* that you created in the Fifth Master Move. Review this completed blueprint often so that the *who, what, why, how, when* and *where* of the success you intend to create is firmly impressed on your mind.

Also when you look ahead and visualise yourself performing, ask yourself: *Do the moves I see myself making genuinely represent my values? Do I need to map and master any new moves if I really want to embody my Ideal Self?* When you look back on what you have done each day, ask yourself: *Did I live out my values today? Was I courageous enough in expressing my Ideal Self?*

When you truly become your Ideal Self, who you are is reflected in what you do. You have a definite identity that resounds within you and radiates out for all to see. The moves you make flow from deep within you and become a natural extension and expression of your time-honoured values. When opportunity presents itself, and success comes knocking on your door, you will be *well poised in a position of power, strength and knowledge* to take advantage – by doing what you love and that which you do best. As the philosopher Aristotle said, "We are what we repeatedly do. Excellence then, is not an act, but a habit."

It is with this thought in mind that I leave you with a story that a great teacher once told me that captures the essence of the Inspired Movement journey. A King made a promise to all his subjects that the person with the most beautiful garden in the kingdom would be blessed with untold riches. Everyone grew excited at the prospect and began cleaning up and bettering their gardens. However, for years the King made no obvious sign of visiting his subjects and seeing the work they had done, and nearly all of them lost faith in his promise and let their gardens go. Unbeknown to them, one day the King disguised himself so that he would not be spotted and made a visit to each garden. He discovered that only one remained in a beautiful state. The King did away with his disguise and approached the man who had fashioned it with such skill and beauty and asked, "How did you manage to keep faith in my promise and create such a wonderful garden?"

"It was easy," replied the man, "I didn't give your rewards a second thought. I simply did what I loved doing – bringing out the best in my garden."

"And now, after I have conferred upon you great riches, what will you do?" asked the King.

The man smiled and said, "I will do what I have always done. I will go on cultivating my garden. I will do my best to make it more beautiful. I will see what greater secrets it has yet to reveal."

---

[1] Hunter-Gault, C., *Fifty Years after the Birmingham Children's Crusade,* The New Yorker, 2 May 2013

[2] A transcript of this speech is available online at: http://www.theguardian.com/theguardian/2007/apr/20/greatspeeches3

[3] Younge, G., *Great Speeches: Its brilliance was in its simplicity,* The Guardian 28 April 2007.

[4] Usain Bolt's comments are from a BBC interview just after the 100m race at the London 2012 Olympics. See: http://www.bbc.co.uk/sport/0/olympics/19137390

[5] McCormack, M., *What they don't teach you at Harvard Business School,* London, Profile Books, 2003 (first published in 1984).

[6] Pele quote taken from an interview he did for the Sky Sports programme: *Football's Greatest – Pele.*

[7] McRae, D., *I'm striving for something I'll never achieve - I'm a mess,* The Guardian, 28 October 2008.

[8] Gardner, H., *Leading Minds,* New York, Basic Books, 2011, p.199.

[9] Schama, S., *The lost art of great speechmaking,* The Guardian, 20 April 2007

[10] See Fox Sport's website: http://msn.foxsports.com/golf/story/Adam-Scott-Ernie-Els-British-Open-072212

[11] Ariely, D., Gneezy, U., Loewenstein, G., & Mazar, N., *Large Stakes and Big Mistakes,* The Review of Economic Studies 76, vol.2 (2009), 451-469.

[12] Ariely, D., *The Upside of Irrationality,* London, Harper, 2011, p31.

[13] The original version of the Yerkes-Dodson Law, also shows that hyperarousal does not adversely impact the performance of simple tasks. See the graph below:

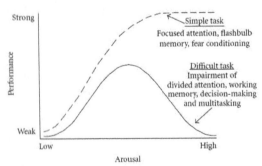

Source: http://en.wikipedia.org/wiki/File:OriginalYerkesDodson.JPG

[14] The quote is attributed to Mo Farah's coach, Alberto Salazar, in the article, *Mo-tivator: How Mo Farah's coach trained him for a double Olympic gold success,* The London Evening Standard, 13 August 2012.

[15] Robertson, I., *The Winner Effect,* London, Bloomsbury, 2012, p203.

[16] Robertson, I., *The Winner Effect,* London, Bloomsbury, 2012, p203.

[17] The adverse effects of the stress or fight-or-flight response are described in: Hallowell, E.M., *Overloaded Circuits in HBR 10 Must Reads: On Managing Yourself,* Boston, Harvard Business Review Press, 2010, p74 and Goleman, D., *The New Leaders,* London, Time Warner, 2005, p27.

[18] The human body, in fact, has three strands to what is known as the autonomic nervous system. In addition to the parasympathetic nervous system and the sympathetic nervous system, there is also the enteric nervous system. A good description of these systems can be found in any human anatomy and physiology textbook, however a good and easy-to-read description of the PNS and SNS is provided in: Hanson, R., with Medius, R., *Buddha's Brain,* Oakland, New Harbinger Publications, 2009, p49-63.

[19] McCraty, R., Atkinson M., and Tomasino, D., *Science of the Heart,* HeartMath Publication, Institute of HeartMath, 2001, p17.

[20] Taken from the Sports Illustrated feature on Maurice Green by Tim Layden, 28 June 1999. Available online at: http://sportsillustrated.cnn.com/olympics/news/2000/02/25/greene_flashback/

[21] Usain Bolt's comments are taken from his interview with the magazine Shortlist: http://www.shortlist.com/entertainment/sport/usain-bolt-interview

[22] Syed, M., *Bounce,* London, Fourth Estate, p185-186.

[23] Hanson, R., with Medius, R., *Buddha's Brain,* Oakland, New Harbinger Publications, 2009. p59.

[24] Csikszentmihalyi, M., *Creativity,* New York, Harper Perennial, 1997, p118-119.

[25] Jackson, P., *Sacred Hoops,* New York, Hyperion, 2006, p18.

[26] *Tao Te Ching* translated by Stephen Mitchell, London, Frances Lincoln Limited, 1999.

[27] Sadler-Smith, E., & Shefy, E., *The intuitive executive: Understanding and applying 'gut feel' in decision-making,* Academy of Management Executive, 2004, Vol.18, No.4.

[28] Coyle, D., *The Talent Code,* London, Arrow Books, p112

[29] Lewis, M.D., *Self-organizing individual differences in brain development,* Development Review, 2005, 25: 252-277.

[30] McCraty, R., Atkinson M., and Tomasino, D., *Science of the Heart,* HeartMath Publication, Institute of HeartMath, 2001, p21.

[31] See: http://www.heartmath.com/personal-use/developing-your-intuition.html

[32] Goleman, D., *The New Leaders,* London, Time Warner Paperbacks, 2005, p54-55.

[33] Whilst many psychologists believe that expert-intuition is nothing more and nothing less than being able to access the accumulated information that is stored

in our memory, others suggest that intuition involves tapping into a higher intelligence or greater capability *beyond* ourselves. For example, many spiritual traditions speak of a Universal Mind or an Infinite Intelligence that we can connect to and access when our conscious minds are in a restful or quiescent state. In fact, many scientifically validated research studies carried out by the Institute of HeartMath scientists we referred to earlier, appear to suggest that we are able to intuitively access information that cannot be attributed to subconsciously stored memories or experiences, leading them to believe that our bodies are "connected by sensory perception to a field of energy that enfolds the information we attribute to intuition". My own subjective experiences of intuition (and from the many stories my clients have narrated to me of correct hunches or series of coincidences that appear to more than just chance happenings) suggest that a greater intelligence works within and around us, which we can beneficially tap into when our conscious minds become relaxed and at ease.

[34] Klein, G., Wolf, S., Militello, L., & Zsambok, C.E., *Characteristics of skilled option generation in chess,* Organisation Behaviour and Human Decision Processes, 1995, 62, 63-69.

[35] Johnston, J., Driskell, J.E., & Salas, E., *Vigilant and hyper vigilant decision making,* Journal of Applied Psychology, 82 1997, 82, 614 - 622.

[36] Sadler-Smith, E., & Shefy, E., *The intuitive executive: Understanding and applying 'gut feel' in decision-making,* Academy of Management Executive, 2004, Vol.18, No.4.

[37] Bill Clinton quoted in Remnick, D., *The Wanderer,* The New Yorker, September 18, 2006, 65.

[38] Klein, G.A., Calderwood, R., & Clinton-Cirocco, A., *Rapid decision making on the fire-ground,* Proceedings of the Human Factors and Ergonomics Society 30th Annual Meeting, 1986, 1, 576-580.

[39] The Guardian Online, *How to be the best kicker in the world,* 5 October 2003: http://www.theguardian.com/sport/2003/oct/05/rugbyworldcup2003.rugbyunion 13

[40] Gardner, H., *Leading Minds,* New York, Basic Books, 2011, p.194-195.

[41] Gardner, H., *Leading Minds,* New York, Basic Books, 2011, p.204.

[42] Schama, S., *The lost art of great speechmaking,* The Guardian, 20 April 2007

[43] The transcript of Nelson Mandela's statement is available at: http://www.theguardian.com/world/2007/apr/23/nelsonmandela2

[44] Ayrton Senna quoted in: Collings, T., & Edworthy, S., *The "Daily Telegraph" Formula One Years,* London, Carlton Books, 2002, p238.

[45] Goleman, D., *The New Leaders,* London, Time Warner Paperbacks, 2005, p131.

[46] Williams, M., & Penman, D., *Mindfulness,* London, Piatkus, p135.

Master Move Exercises

* The exercises within the morning preview and evening review are listed in the order in which they are to be performed.

Morning Preview Exercise *

1. Concentration countdown – **Master Move 6**

2. Entering the optimal inner state of dynamic poise – **Master Move 7**

3. Seeing yourself performing at your best – **Master Move 3**

4. Seeing and feeling the future with enhanced belief – **Master Move 4**

    (With greater belief, I am more...)

5. Seeing your precise moves of success – **Master Move 5**

    (Visualising your Inspired Movement Success Blueprint)

6. Contemplating the day ahead – **Master Move 6**

    (What is likely to happen today? What would happen if...?)

7. Checking your alignment with the Ideal Way Forward – **Master Move 7**

    (Do the moves I see myself making today represent my defining values?)

Evening Review Exercise *

1. Concentration countdown – **Master Move 6**

2. Entering into the optimal inner state of dynamic poise – **Master Move 7**

3. Refining the Ideal Way Forward – **Master Move 1**

    (What worked? What didn't work? What do I need to change?)

4. Re-living what you loved – **Master Move 3**

    (What did I most love about my work or life today?)

5. An honest appraisal of your Ideal Self – **Master Move 4**

    (How bold was I today in expressing my Ideal Self? Could I have achieved more with greater courage?)

Master Move Exercises

6. Refining your mental model of important situations – **Master Move 6**

   (Has anything I have learnt today changed my perspective in any way?)

7. Checking your alignment with the Ideal Way Forward – **Master Move 7**

   (Did I live out my values today?)

Knowing your Ideal Way Forward

1. Seeing what you desire above all else – **Master Move 2**

2. Writing your autobiography – **Master Move 2**

3. Connecting your purpose and your ruling passion – **Master Move 3**

4. Mapping, chunking, and mastering your optimal moves –

   Master Move 5 *(Creating your Inspired Movement Success Blueprint)*

5. Seeking out your mentor – **Master Move 6**

Knowing your Ideal Self

1. Enhancing your belief and presence – **Master Move 4**

   (If I really believe in myself what more is possible?)

2. Moving, feeling, and thinking like an Inspired Mover you admire –

   Master Move 6

3. Tuning into your inner state – **Master Move 7**

   (What am I thinking and feeling? The ABC model of emotions)

4. Affirming your three defining values – **Master Move 7**

   (Who do you choose to be?)

Index

Index

Index

Index

Index

Index

Other Books from Bennion Kearny

José Mourinho: The Rise of the Translator by Ciaran Kelly

From Porto to Chelsea, and Inter to Real Madrid – the Mourinho story is as intriguing as the man himself. Now, a new challenge awaits at Stamford Bridge. Covering the Mourinho story to October 2013 and featuring numerous exclusive interviews with figures not synonymous with the traditional Mourinho narrative.

"Enlightening interviews with those who really know José Mourinho" – Simon Kuper, Financial Times.

"Superb read from a terrific writer" – Ger McCarthy, Irish Examiner

Graduation: Life Lessons of a Professional Footballer by Richard Lee

The 2010/11 season will go down as a memorable one for Goalkeeper Richard Lee. Cup wins, penalty saves, hypnotherapy and injury would follow, but these things only tell a small part of the tale. Filled with anecdotes, insights, humour and honesty - Graduation uncovers Richard's campaign to take back the number one spot, save a lot of penalties, and overcome new challenges. What we see is a transformation - beautifully encapsulated in this extraordinary season.

Golf Tough: Practice, Prepare, Perform and Progress
by Dan Abrahams

Dan Abrahams is Lead Psychologist for England Golf, as well as a former touring professional golfer, and PGA coach. In Golf Tough, Dan offers you a powerful blueprint for improvement and a detailed plan for consistent high performance no matter what your standard of play. If you want to significantly lower your handicap, compete with greater consistency, win tournaments or reach the next level on the course, Dan's simple yet powerful philosophies, tools and techniques will help you break through your current barriers and reach your golfing goals.

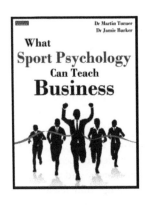

What Sport Psychology Can Teach Business: Ten Lessons for Peak Professional Performance
by Dr Martin Turner & Dr Jamie Barker

It goes without saying that business performance has many parallels with sporting performance. But did you realize that the scientific principles of sport psychology, used by elite athletes the world over, are being used by some of the most successful business professionals? Performance - in any context - is about utilizing and deploying every possible resource to fulfil your potential.

With this book you will develop the most important weapon you need to succeed in business: your mental approach to performance. This book reveals the secrets of the winning mind by exploring the strategies and techniques used by the most successful athletes and professionals on the planet.

Lightning Source UK Ltd.
Milton Keynes UK
UKHW02f0612091018
330241UK00009B/350/P